BARBECUE RECIPES: BBQ CO
BEGINNERS AND EX

SIMPLE GUIDE TO MAKE RECIPES FOR BARBECUE TO MAKE AMAZING MEALS WITH YOUR FAMILY AND FRIENDS

By

Roberto DEL RIO

TABLE OF CONTENS

INTRODUCTION

Cooking with barbecue o BBQ

How can you resist a nice barbecue of meat, fish or vegetables, to be enjoyed with friends?The Barbecue gives to the dishes a special taste, with an irresistible external crunchiness, whether it is charcoal or gas the secret of the barbecue is the temperature and the cooking time. Those who do not live in the countryside or in a house with a garden will be able to enjoy a barbecue with friends thanks to the portable barbecue suitable for the city.

Which barbecue to choose:

WOOD-FIRED BARBECUE

The most traditional barbecue is definitely the wood-fired one. It has a special charm, because it is one of the oldest cooking techniques. It may seem simple, but it requires some experience to achieve optimal cooking results. The wood fired barbecue is quite difficult to light and it needs a constant control and a longer time, in fact it takes about 30 minutes before it is ready to start cooking. Cooking over embers gives the food a strong flavor; the heat that is obtained by using wood reaches high peaks and decreases during cooking.

GAS BARBECUE

The gas barbecue is modern and more technical than the wood barbecue. The gas barbecue works like any stove or oven at home. It is very practical, turns on with a button and is ready in minutes. It provides an even and constant spread of heat and allows you to adjust the temperature with ease.

Portable barbecue

ELECTRIC BARBECUE

The electric barbecue is practical and easy to use. It is especially ideal for those who live in the city or for camping. The advantages of the electric barbecue are the minimal smoke production, with a constant even heat spread, and easy temperature control.

CHOOSING THE MEAT FOR THE BARBECUE

How do you decide which meat to choose? The choice of meat for the barbecue depends on personal taste and budget. You can cook on the barbecue: beef, pork, chicken, veal, lamb, etc.

Beef is the perfect meat for barbecuing because it withstands high temperatures very well. Which cut to choose for the barbecue? The fillet is more tender but less flavorful, the sirloin, to be cooked whole on the barbecue and cut into slices after cooking, is tastier.

Another meat that cannot miss on the barbecue is pork, ribs and tips. The pieces should not be too lean, because it is precisely the fat that makes them more tender and juicy.

BARBECUE WITH LAMB IS TYPICAL OF THE EASTER PERIOD

Another classic that can not miss on the barbecue? Salamelle and sausages, a must for barbecue cooking.

Are skewers also perfect for the barbecue? Delicious and also scenic, you must be careful in assembling them, using pieces of meat and vegetables that have similar cooking times.

PREPARATION AND COOKING WITH THE BARBECUE:

Salt the meat: generally, meat should be salted after cooking, never long before, because salt removes the water causing it to harden. But for barbecue cooking, salting a moment before putting the meat on the grill helps the formation of the crust and enhances the flavor. Don't Prick: Poking the meat disperses its cooking juices and therefore, in addition to the flavor, the nutrients.

Cooking times: the beef should be placed on the barbecue first so that it can form a crispy crust and leave the inside rare. Next, put the sausages and last the lamb and other meats that cook at lower temperatures. Bone-in chicken and turkey pieces should be cooked on the outermost parts of the grill, with indirect heat. Before serving: Beef should be removed from the heat and allowed to rest in a dish covered with aluminum foil to maintain heat, so when serving it will be softer.

BARBECUE COOKING TIMES

Sausages: 10-15 minutes
Ribs: 45 minutes
Chops: 5 minutes per side
Skewers: 15-20 minutes
Fish: (about 1 kg) 20 minutes
Thighs: 25-30 minutes
Skewers: 15-20 minutes
Crustaceans: 3 minutes
Beef steak: 2-3 minutes per side
Veal chops: 5 minutes per side
Cheese: 1 minute
Chops: 5 minutes per side
Fruits and vegetables: no more than 7 minutes

NOT A CARNIVORE?

You can also cook vegetables on the barbecue as a side dish or as a main course if you don't eat meat. The important thing is to choose vegetables according to their thickness and cooking time, and cook them at a lower temperature than meat to prevent them from becoming mushy and charred. The ideal thickness of the slices for cooking vegetables on the barbecue is about 1 cm. Cooking fish on the barbecue is faster than meat and at a lower temperature. Fish should be marinated before cooking them on the barbeque, or cooked in aluminum foil to retain moisture inside the fish. Fish steaks should always be cooked with the skin side down for even cooking and to make the skin crispy and golden.

MARINADES

How to marinate meat For a perfect barbecue, marinating meat is important. The meat becomes tender and flavorful and the marinade enriches it with the beneficial properties of the herbs and spices you choose.

To marinate meat it is necessary to prepare an emulsion based on extra virgin olive oil and lemon juice, to which you can add spices and aromatic herbs rich in antioxidants: sage, rosemary, oregano, thyme, chili pepper, basil, mint, garlic, tarragon possibly fresh. Marinating must be done in the refrigerator and requires different times depending on the type of meat: from 4 to 6 hours of marinating for red meat, from 2 to 4 hours of marinating for pork and poultry, from 30 minutes to 2 hours of marinating for fish.

MARINADE FOR MEAT

To make the best marinade, you can use food bags. Pour the marinade inside, one coffee cup for every 200 grams of meat. Place the pieces of meat in the bag, close and let rest in the refrigerator for the time required by the type of meat. The marinade should also be used to brush the meat during cooking, turning it often; it should never be used to flavor meat once it is cooked: the marinade remaining after cooking must be thrown away. It is important to bring the meat to room temperature before cooking it.

MARINADE FOR VEGETABLES

Marinating is essential when cooking grilled vegetables. There are many variants, but the most common is obtained by simply mixing oil, vinegar, garlic, salt and pepper. Other ingredients and flavors can be added according to personal taste. Once ready, marinade should be left to rest for a while in order to amalgamate ingredients. In the meantime clean and slice the vegetables and brush them with the marinade. Spennerl with the marinade before and during cooking, every time the pieces are turned. Once cooked, it is a good idea to brush them with a little more marinade before serving.

MARINADE FOR FISH

Combine 1 tablespoon lemon juice, 3 tablespoons extra virgin olive oil, sea salt, freshly ground black pepper, and finely chopped parsley, rosemary, sage and dried garlic. Brush the fish with the marinade several times, starting at least an hour before grilling and during cooking.

HOW TO MARINATE TO PERFECTION:

Marinating consists of three elements: an acid, an oil and spices or herbs. The oily element: extra virgin olive oil is the perfect base The acidic element: for chicken and lamb lemon is used, for beef vinegar, wine or beer is used.

The spices or aromatic herbs: rosemary and thyme are useful against harmful substances which would develop during grilling. Doses: the right proportion for a perfect marinade is one part fat or oil and two parts acid, with the addition of aromas as desired. Rub

BARBECUE SAUCES AND RUBS

At the end of cooking, to accompany and add flavor to the meat cooked on the barbecue, you can prepare sauces. The most classic, with an unmistakable taste, is the American barbecue sauce, capable of transforming ribs and other grilled meats into real masterpieces, but there are many recipes, for example with cucumber, radish, mayonnaise, onion... there is something for every taste.

CLASSIC BARBECUE SAUCE RECIPE

- 200 g of tomato sauce - 1 tablespoon of tomato paste - 1 yellow onion - 1 garlic clove - 3 tablespoons of white vinegar - 2 tablespoons of mustard - 2 tablespoons of sugar - 1 hot pepper - 20 g of butter - Tabasco sauce to taste. - Worcester sauce to taste - salt and pepper to taste.

Finely chop the onion and garlic and brown in a pan with the butter over high heat, deglaze with vinegar. Add the tomato puree and tomato paste, add the mustard, chili pepper and sugar, mix well. Cook the barbecue sauce for about twenty minutes, remove from heat and allow to cool. Strain through a sieve and adjust salt and pepper, and add a few drops of Tabasco and Worcester sauce to taste.

THE GUACAMOLE SAUCE

- 2 large avocados - 2-3 cherry tomatoes - 1 small red onion - the juice of 1 lime - salt and pepper to taste - 3 tablespoons extra virgin olive oil - a few chopped fresh coriander leaves.

Scoop out the pulp from the avocados, cut it into small pieces and lightly mash it in a bowl. Add the chopped tomatoes, onion, chopped coriander leaves, oil, lime juice, salt and pepper and mix well.

RUB OR DRY MARINADE

Rub, also called "dry marinade", is a mixture of spices and flavorings to be rubbed on food before cooking. It takes its name from the gesture of rubbing, rub in English. Here are some basic mixtures: combine the ingredients by mixing them well and rub them in before cooking.

RUB FOR MEAT

- 2 tablespoons sweet paprika - 3 tablespoons coarse salt - 2 tablespoons brown sugar - 3 tablespoons ground black pepper - 1 tablespoon smoked salt - 1 teaspoon cayenne pepper - 2 teaspoons celery seeds - 2 teaspoons garlic - 2 teaspoons onion powder

RUB FOR FISH

- 3 tablespoons coarse salt - 2 tablespoons brown sugar - 1 tablespoon black pepper powder - 1 tablespoon dill - 1 teaspoon mustard - 2 teaspoons garlic - 2 teaspoons onion powder

RUB FOR VEGETABLES

- 2 teaspoons of ground fennel seeds - 3 teaspoons of coarse salt - 3 teaspoons of chili powder - 2 teaspoons of celery seeds - 1 teaspoon of black pepper powder - grated peel of 2 lemons

AUTHOR'S NOTE: We would like to thank TESCOMA SPA (TESCOMA ON LINE) for collaboration to the book introduction. TESCOMA SPA, Via Traversa Caduti del Lavoro n.3 -24056 CAZZAGO S.MARTINO(BS) – ITALY

1 RELIABLE ASADO BBQ WITH RED CHILI SAUCE

Servings: 8 **Cook Time: 20 Min** **Prep Time 1 H**

INGREDIENTS:

PREPARE RED CHILI SAUCE:
- ✓ 1/2 teaspoon black pepper
- ✓ 1/2 teaspoon salt
- ✓ About 1 teaspoon ground cumin
- ✓ 1/2 teaspoon minced garlic

PREPARE PORK:
- ✓ 1 cup flour
- ✓ About 1 teaspoon ground cumin
- ✓ 1 medium onion (Chopped)
- ✓ 1/2 teaspoon ground black pepper About
- ✓ 1 teaspoon Mexican oregano

- ✓ 7 cup water
- ✓ About 1 teaspoon Mexican oregano
- ✓ 13 dried chili pods

- ✓ 1/2 cup canola oil
- ✓ 1/2 teaspoon salt
- ✓ 1/2 teaspoon chopped garlic
- ✓ 4 lb pork roast

DIRECTIONS:

- ➤ First of all, please assemble all the ingredients at one place
- ➤ To make the sauce combine all the chili sauce ingredients. Mix well.
- ➤ Then add to a pot & heat until it gets thickened.
- ➤ This step is important. Cut the pork into small pieces.

- ➤ Combine the Mexican oregano, canola oil, salt, garlic, oil, flour, cumin, black pepper and mix well.
- ➤ One thing remains to be done
- ➤ Now add the pork pieces & marinate for 1 hour.
- ➤ Finally preheat the grill & grill the pork for about 2 to 5 minutes on each side.

2 CHARMING APPLE BUTTER AND FIREBALL BBQ SAUCE

Servings: 3 Cups **Cook Time: 50 Min** **Prep Time 1 H**

INGREDIENTS:

- ✓ 1 teaspoon salt
- ✓ 1/2 yellow onion (Diced)
- ✓ 3 garlic cloves (Minced)
- ✓ About 1.5 teaspoon ground black pepper
- ✓ 1 1/2 cups apple butter
- ✓ About 1/2 cup cinnamon whiskey, such as Fireball
- ✓ 1 teaspoon ground mustard

- ✓ 1/2 cup ketchup
- ✓ 1/3 cup apple cider vinegar
- ✓ About 1.5 teaspoon cayenne pepper flakes
- ✓ 1/2 cup brown sugar, packed
- ✓ 2 tablespoons Worcestershire sauce
- ✓ 1 tablespoon olive oil

DIRECTIONS:

- ➤ First of all, please assemble all the ingredients at one place
- ➤ Coat the bottom of a saucepan with the oil.
- ➤ Then add the garlic and onion & place on the stove over medium heat, sautéing the onions until they become translucent.
- ➤ Pour the cinnamon whiskey into the saucepan with the tender vegetables & stir until well combined.
- ➤ This step is important
- ➤ Next, please bring the mixture to a boil before reducing the heat & simmering for about 10 to 15 minutes, while stirring frequently.
- ➤ Now while the mixture is simmering

- ➤ Combine the ketchup, apple butter, vinegar, Worcestershire sauce, mustard, brown sugar, black pepper, salt, & cayenne pepper in a mixing bowl.
- ➤ Combine the two mixture.
- ➤ Then turn the heat up & bring the mixture back to a boil, while stirring regularly.
- ➤ Once it boils, reduce the heat again & let it simmer for about 25 to 30 minutes.
- ➤ One thing remains to be done. Next, please remove the saucepan from the heat & let it cool down.
- ➤ Finally use immediately or pour into mason jars & store in the fridge until ready to use.

3 BBQ ROAST WITH ONIONS

Servings: 4   **Cook Time: 10 Min**   **Prep Time 12 Min**

INGREDIENTS:
- ✓ 1 to 2 Medium Tomatoes
- ✓ 1 Shallot
- ✓ 60 ml of Red Wine Vinegar
- ✓ 2 Tablespoons of Fresh Chopped Marjoram
- ✓ 1 Tablespoon of Fresh Chopped Rosemary
- ✓ 1 Teaspoon of Salt
- ✓ ½ Teaspoon of Freshly Ground Pepper
- ✓ 1 ½ Pounds of Flank Steak

DIRECTIONS:
- ➢ Mix altogether in a blender
- ➢ Place the tomato with the shallot, the rosemary, the marjoram, the salt
- ➢ Add the pepper; then blend very well together
- ➢ Blend your ingredients until they form a paste
- ➢ Set it aside for about 4 hours in the refrigerator in a sealable plastic bag where you put the meat with it
- ➢ Heat up the grill and set it above the heat at a height that cooks the meat

- ➢ Make sure to oil the rack
- ➢ Then once the barbecue is heated up very well
- ➢ Set up your grill over the heat
- ➢ Grill for about 4 to 5 minutes per side
- ➢ At this point brush with more puree
- ➢ Remove from the heat when you finish to a clean plate
- ➢ Let rest for about 5 minutes; then serve and enjoy your dish!

4 BBQ BEEF MEATBALLS

Servings: 2   **Cook Time: 25 Min**   **Prep Time 15 Min**

INGREDIENTS:
- ✓ 1 Pound of Ground Beef
- ✓ 1 Large Onion, chopped into pieces of 1 inch each
- ✓ 1 Large cut into pieces of
- ✓ 1 inch each red bell pepper
- ✓ 1 Cup of dried Bread Crumbs
- ✓ 60ml of Milk
- ✓ 1 Cup of grated Parmesan cheese

- ✓ 2 Minced garlic Gloves Garlic
- ✓ 2 Tablespoons of Dried Parsley
- ✓ 1 Tablespoon of Dried Basil
- ✓ ½ Teaspoon of Salt
- ✓ ½ Teaspoon of Black Pepper
- ✓ 2 Large Eggs

DIRECTIONS:
- ➢ In a small bowl; combine the breadcrumbs and the milk and set aside for 5 minutes
- ➢ Squeeze the bread crumbs so that you can remove any excess of milk
- ➢ Then combine the cheese, the beef, the herbs, the salt, the pepper and the eggs
- ➢ Mix your ingredients very well together;
- ➢ Shape the meat into meatballs of about ½ inch each ball

- ➢ Place the meatballs onto skewers
- ➢ Make sure to place a piece of pepper and a piece of onion
- ➢ Put the kebabs on the grill
- ➢ Grill for about 10 minutes; rotate every 2 to 3 minutes
- ➢ Remove from the heat; then serve and enjoy your dish!

5 ROUND EYE STEAKS

Servings: 3 **Cook Time: 15 Min** **Prep Time 10 Min**

INGREDIENTS:

- ✓ 1 Pound of Round Eye Steaks (1 inch of thickness)
- ✓ The Juice of 1 Lime
- ✓ 1 Teaspoon of Garlic Powder
- ✓ 1 Teaspoon of Cumin Powder
- ✓ 1 Teaspoon of Ground Coriander
- ✓ 1 Teaspoon of Salt
- ✓ 1 Teaspoon of Freshly Ground Pepper

DIRECTIONS:

- ➤ Combine the lime juice with the garlic powder, the cumin, the coriander and the pepper
- ➤ Make sure to trim any quantity of fats that you can see on the steaks
- ➤ Then place in a plastic bag that can be sealed
- ➤ Pour in the mixture you have made earlier on the steaks
- ➤ Leave in the refrigerator for about 30 minutes
- ➤ Heat up the grill for about 15 minutes
- ➤ Remove the steaks from the heat and let rest for about 5 minutes
- ➤ Serve and enjoy your dish!

6 STRIP STEAK WITH OREGANO AND GARLIC

Servings: 4 **Cook Time: 8 Min** **Prep Time 5 Min**

INGREDIENTS:

- ✓ 4 Strip Steaks, of about
- ✓ 1 Inch of thickness
- ✓ 3 Minced garlic Gloves
- ✓ 1 and ½ Tablespoons of Olive Oil
- ✓ 1 Tablespoon of Dried Crushed Oregano
- ✓ ¼ Teaspoon of Salt
- ✓ ¼ Teaspoon of Freshly Ground Pepper

DIRECTIONS:

- ➤ In a medium bowl; combine all together the oil with the garlic, the oregano, the salt and the
- ➤ Then sprinkle on both sides of the meat
- ➤ Place the meat in a dish; then cover
- ➤ Put in the refrigerator for about 2 to 3 hours to marinate
- ➤ Heat the barbecue for about 10 minutes
- ➤ Grill each side of the meat for about 6 to 8 minutes
- ➤ Once both sides have perfectly cooked to your liking
- ➤ Remove from the heat; then let rest for about 5 minutes
- ➤ Serve and enjoy your dish!

7 BEEF BURGERS

Servings: 5 **Cook Time: 10 Min** **Prep Time 10 Min**

INGREDIENTS:

- ✓ 1 Pounds of Lean Ground Beef
- ✓ 1 Pack of Ranch Dressing Mix
- ✓ 1 Lightly beaten egg
- ✓ ¼ Pound of crushed Saltine Crackers
- ✓ 1 Finely chopped onion

DIRECTIONS:

- ➤ Place the ground beef with the dressing mix, the egg, the crushed
- ➤ Add crackers and the onion in a bowl and mix very well
- ➤ Combine your ingredients very well
- ➤ Then turn form into hamburger patties
- ➤ Heat your Barbecue for about 5 minutes
- ➤ At this point once the barbecue has reached the desired heat
- ➤ Place the burgers on the grill
- ➤ Cook the burgers for about 5 minutes per side
- ➤ Serve the burgers in sesame topped buns
- ➤ Serve and enjoy your burgers!

8 A VERY POPULAR BBQ SAUCE

Servings: 32   **Cook Time: 10 Min**   **Prep Time 10 Min**

INGREDIENTS:

- ✓ 1 1/2 cups brown sugar
- ✓ 1 1/2 cups ketchup
- ✓ 1/2 cup red wine vinegar
- ✓ 1/2 cup water
- ✓ 1 tbsp. Worcestershire sauce

- ✓ 2 1/2 tbsps. dry mustard
- ✓ 2 tsps. paprika
- ✓ 2 tsps. salt
- ✓ 1 1/2 tsps. black pepper
- ✓ 2 dashes hot pepper sauce

DIRECTIONS:

- ➤ Mix together Worcestershire sauce, water, vinegar, ketchup, and brown sugar in a blender

- ➤ Add hot pepper sauce, pepper, salt, paprika, and mustard for seasoning
- ➤ Process until no lumps remain.

9 ABSOLUTELY ULTIMATE MARINADE

Servings: 16   **Cook Time: 5 Min**   **Prep Time 10 Min**

INGREDIENTS:

- ✓ 2 tbsps. sesame seeds
- ✓ 1 bunch green onions, chopped
- ✓ 8 cloves garlic, minced
- ✓ 2 tbsps. tahini

- ✓ 1/2 cup soy sauce
- ✓ 1/2 cup white sugar
- ✓ 1/4 cup red wine vinegar
- ✓ 1/2 tsp. freshly ground black pepper

DIRECTIONS:

- ➤ In a dry skillet, place the sesame seeds on medium heat
- ➤ Then cook while stirring until fragrant and golden brown, about 5 minutes.
- ➤ Mix together pepper, red wine vinegar, white sugar, soy sauce

- ➤ Add tahini, garlic, green onions, and toasted sesame seeds in a medium bowl
- ➤ Place the meat you want to use into the mixture
- ➤ Marinate, covered, as long as you like
- ➤ It is best to marinate overnight. As desired, grill the meat.

10 ALL PURPOSE LIME MARINADE

Servings: 4   **Cook Time: 0 Min**   **Prep Time 10 Min**

INGREDIENTS:

- ✓ 1/3 cup freshly squeezed lime juice
- ✓ 2 tbsps. teriyaki sauce
- ✓ 2 green

- ✓ 2 tbsps. minced fresh ginger root
- ✓ 1/4 tsp. ancho chile powder

DIRECTIONS:

- ➤ To prepare marinade, whisk ancho powder, ginger
- ➤ Add green onions, teriyaki sauce, and lime juice together.

- ➤ For using, marinate your preferred meat for 2-4 hours
- ➤ Then grill over hardwood charcoal.

11 ALL-AROUND SPICE RUB

Servings: 12   **Cook Time: 0 Min**   **Prep Time 5 Min**

INGREDIENTS:

- ✓ 3/4 cup paprika
- ✓ 1/4 cup fresh-ground pepper blend
- ✓ 1/4 cup dark brown sugar
- ✓ 2 tbsps. chili powder

- ✓ 2 tbsps. garlic powder
- ✓ 2 tbsps. onion powder
- ✓ 1 tbsp. sea salt
- ✓ 2 tsps. cayenne pepper

DIRECTIONS:

- ➤ In a lidded container, stir together cayenne pepper, sea salt

- ➤ Add onion powder, chili powder, brown sugar, pepper and paprika
- ➤ Keep in a cool, dark place between uses.

12 BBQ SPARE RIBS

Servings: 6 **Cook Time: 1 H 30 Min** **Prep Time 5 Min**

INGREDIENTS:

- ✓ 5 ½ Pounds of Pork Spare Ribs
- ✓ 240ml of Ready Made Barbecue Sauce

DIRECTIONS:

- ➢ Start by placing the ribs over a low heat on your barbecue
- ➢ Then cook for about 1 and ½ hours
- ➢ About 15 minutes before removing the pork from the barbecue
- ➢ Start brushing with the barbecue sauce
- ➢ Turn the ribs over and make sure to baste with the sauce regularly
- ➢ And as soon as the ribs are cooking; remove it from the barbecue and cut it up into portions
- ➢ Serve and enjoy with coleslaw of your choice!

13 BOURBON PORK RIBS

Servings: 6 **Cook Time: 45Min** **Prep Time 5 Min**

INGREDIENTS:

- ✓ 3 Pounds of Country style Pork Ribs
- ✓ 1 Cup of Dark Brown Sugar
- ✓ 240ml of Light Soy Sauce
- ✓ 150ml of Bourbon
- ✓ 4 Minced Garlic Cloves

DIRECTIONS:

- ➢ In a blender or a food processor; put the sugar with the soy sauce, the garlic and the bourbon
- ➢ Blend until you get a fully combined mixture
- ➢ Cover the pork ribs with the prepared marinade
- ➢ Then let refrigerate for several hours
- ➢ Preheat your barbecue for about 7 minutes
- ➢ Then remove the meat from the refrigerator and let come to the room temperature; and brush with oil
- ➢ Place the pork ribs on the grills of the barbecue and close the lid
- ➢ Cook for about 1 hour and 45 minutes
- ➢ Remove the pork from the barbecue and let rest for about 5 minutes, Serve and enjoy with salads and potatoes!

14 GLAZED MARINATED PORK

Servings: 3 **Cook Time: 75Min** **Prep Time 8 Min**

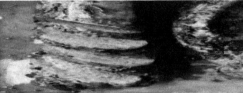

INGREDIENTS:

- ✓ 4 Boneless Pork Loin Chops of about
- ✓ 1 inch of thickness 160ml of Orange Marmalade
- ✓ 1 Finely chopped Jalapeno Pepper, Seeded
- ✓ 2 Tablespoons of Lime Juice or Tequila
- ✓ 1 Teaspoon of Freshly Grated Ginger

DIRECTIONS:

- ➢ Combine in a bowl the jalapeño pepper with the lime juice or the tequila and the ginger
- ➢ Make sure to trim any fat off the meat
- ➢ Heat the barbecue for about 10 minutes
- ➢ Barbecue the pork chops for about 12 to 15 minutes
- ➢ Make sure to baste the pork chops regularly when you cook it and during the last five minutes
- ➢ Make sure to apply the glaze very often
- ➢ Once the pork chops are perfectly barbecued
- ➢ Remove the pork from the heat and let cool for about 5 minutes
- ➢ Sprinkle with the fresh and chopped cilantro
- ➢ Serve and enjoy with orange and lime wedges!

15 PORK SATAY

Servings: 3 **Cook Time: 5Min** **Prep Time 6 Min**

INGREDIENTS:
- ✓ 1 Pound of Pork Tenderloin
- ✓ 1 Small finely chopped Onion
- ✓ ½ cup of Brown Sugar
- ✓ 60ml of Water
- ✓ 3 Tablespoons of Reduced Sodium Soy Sauce
- ✓ 2 Tablespoons of Reduced Fat Creamy Peanut Butter
- ✓ 4 ½ Teaspoons of Canola Oil
- ✓ 2 Finely minced Garlic Cloves
- ✓ ¼ Teaspoon of Ground Ginger

DIRECTIONS:
- ➤ Place the onion with the sugar, the peanut butter, the water, the soy sauce
- ➤ Add the canola oil, the garlic and the ginger in a small sauce pan
- ➤ Bring to a boil uncovered for about 10 to 12 minutes
- ➤ Make sure to keep stirring to prevent sticking
- ➤ Cut the pork into half width wise
- ➤ Then cut each into thin strips; then soak into water for about ½ hour
- ➤ Place over an oiled grill on your barbecue to hot heat and barbecue for about 2 to 3 minutes per side
- ➤ Make sure to baste regularly; then transfer the pork cuts to a serving plate and let rest for about 5 minutes
- ➤ Serve and enjoy with a dipping sauce of your choice

16 HONEY MUSTARD BBQ PORK

Servings: 4 **Cook Time: 11Min** **Prep Time 8 Min**

INGREDIENTS:
- ✓ 4 Pork Chops of about
- ✓ ¾ Inch of Thickness
- ✓ 90ml of Honey
- ✓ 3 Tablespoons of Fresh Orange Juice
- ✓ 1 Tablespoon of Cider Vinegar
- ✓ 1 Tablespoon of White Wine
- ✓ 2 Teaspoons of Worcestershire Sauce
- ✓ 2 Teaspoon of Onion Powder
- ✓ ½ Teaspoon of Dried Tarragon
- ✓ 3 Tablespoon of Dijon Mustard

DIRECTIONS:
- ➤ Put the honey in a small bowl
- ➤ Then add in the orange, the honey, the orange, the vinegar
- ➤ Add the wine, the Worcestershire sauce, the onion powder, the tarragon and the mustard
- ➤ Mix very well together; then place to one side
- ➤ Take the pork chops and try to make cuts into the fatty edge of each portion of pork
- ➤ Place the pork meat in a shallow dish
- ➤ At this point pour the marinade over the top and cover
- ➤ Place the meat in the refrigerate for about 2 hours
- ➤ Heat your Barbecue for about 5 to 7 minutes
- ➤ Then place the pork chops on top of the grill
- ➤ Cook for about 3 to 4 minutes per side
- ➤ Remove the meat from the heat and let rest for about 5 minutes
- ➤ Serve and enjoy your dish!

17 LAMB WITH BROWN SUGAR GLAZE

Servings: 7　　　　　**Cook Time: 10 Min**　　　　　**Prep Time 7 Min**

INGREDIENTS:
- ✓ 4 to 5 Lamb Chops
- ✓ 1 Cup of Brown Sugar
- ✓ 2 Teaspoons of Ground Ginger
- ✓ 2 Teaspoons of Dried Tarragon
- ✓ 1 Teaspoon of Ground Cinnamon
- ✓ 1 Teaspoon of Ground Black Pepper
- ✓ 1 Teaspoon of Garlic Powder
- ✓ ½ Teaspoon of Salt

DIRECTIONS:
- ➢ In a large bowl; place the finger with the sugar, the cinnamon
- ➢ Add the pepper, the garlic powder and the salt
- ➢ Mix very well together
- ➢ Take the seasoning mixture
- ➢ Then rub very well into the lamb chops on both the sides of the meat and cover
- ➢ At this point place in the refrigerator for about 1 hour
- ➢ Heat the barbecue for about 5 minutes
- ➢ Remove the lamb chops from the refrigerator
- ➢ Brush your grill with some oil
- ➢ Then lay the lamb chops on the grill
- ➢ Cook the lamb for about 5 minutes per side
- ➢ Serve and enjoy your with a salad of your choice!

18 HERB MARINATED LAMB

Servings: 4　　　　　**Cook Time: 6 Min**　　　　　**Prep Time 15 Min**

INGREDIENTS:
- ✓ 2 Pounds of Lamb Chops
- ✓ 60ml of Distilled White Vinegar
- ✓ 2 Teaspoons of Salt
- ✓ ½ Teaspoon of Ground Black Pepper
- ✓ 1 Tablespoon of Minced Garlic
- ✓ 1 Medium thinly Sliced Onion
- ✓ 2 Tablespoons of Olive Oil

DIRECTIONS:
- ➢ Place the vinegar in a large resealable bag with the salt, the pepper, the garlic
- ➢ Add the onion and the olive oil and shake very well
- ➢ Place the lamb chops in the bag and shake
- ➢ Then let marinate for about 4 hours
- ➢ Remove the lamb meat from the refrigerator; while your barbecue is heating up
- ➢ Arrange the lamb chops on lightly oiled grill
- ➢ Grill for about 3 minutes per side
- ➢ Once perfectly cooked
- ➢ Remove the lamb chops from the heat
- ➢ At this point let rest for 5 minutes
- ➢ Serve and enjoy your dish!

19 BBQ LEG OF LAMB

Servings: 5   **Cook Time: 30 Min**   **Prep Time 6 Min**

INGREDIENTS:

- ✓ 3 Pounds of Boneless Leg of Lamb
- ✓ 1 Cup of Freshly Chopped Cilantro
- ✓ 1 Cup of Freshly Chopped Mint
- ✓ 60ml of Olive Oil
- ✓ 2 Finely minced Garlic Cloves
- ✓ 2 Teaspoons of Ground Coriander
- ✓ 1 Teaspoon of Freshly Grated Ginger
- ✓ 1 Teaspoon of Salt
- ✓ ½ Teaspoon of Chili Powder

DIRECTIONS:

- ➤ In a small bowl; mix the oil with the cilantro, the mint, the garlic
- ➤ Add the mint, the garlic, the coriander, the ginger, the salt and the chilli powder
- ➤ Put the boneless leg of lamb in a shallow dish
- ➤ Then pour the marinade over it; cover with the aluminium foil
- ➤ Place it into the refrigerator to marinate for about 2 hours
- ➤ Remove the meat from the refrigerator
- ➤ At this point heat your BBQ for about 10 minutes
- ➤ Place the lamb over an oiled grill and barbecue for about 20 to 30 minutes
- ➤ Remove from the BBQ
- ➤ Let the meat rest for 5 minutes
- ➤ Serve and enjoy your dish!

20 GREEK-STYLE LAMB CHOPS

Servings: 6   **Cook Time: 17 Min**   **Prep Time 6 Min**

INGREDIENTS:

- ✓ 8 to 9 Lamb Chops
- ✓ 120 ml of Olive Oil
- ✓ 120ml of Red Wine Vinegar
- ✓ 1 Cup of Freshly Chopped Mint
- ✓ 3 Minced garlic Cloves
- ✓ 1 Teaspoon of Salt
- ✓ 1 Teaspoon of Freshly Ground Black Pepper

DIRECTIONS:

- ➤ In a bowl; mix the olive with the red wine vinegar, the freshly
- ➤ Add chopped mint and the minced garlic cloves
- ➤ Pour the mixture into the bag; then coat the meat very well with it
- ➤ Let refrigerate for about 2 hours
- ➤ Remove the meat from the refrigerator
- ➤ Preheat your barbecue for about 10 minutes
- ➤ Sprinkle the salt and the pepper over the meat
- ➤ Place the lamb meat over the grill of the barbecue
- ➤ Cook for about 5 to 6 minutes per side
- ➤ After removing the lamb chops from the refrigerator
- ➤ Should preheat your barbecue for at least 5 to 6 minutes per side
- ➤ Remove the meat from the barbecue; then let rest for about 5 minutes
- ➤ Serve and enjoy your dish with Greek salad!

21 LAMB SKEWERS

Servings: 3   **Cook Time: 10 Min**   **Prep Time 15 Min**

INGREDIENTS:

- ✓ 1 Pound of Diced lean lamb
- ✓ 3 Teaspoons of extra virgin olive oil
- ✓ 3 Crushed garlic cloves
- ✓ 2 Teaspoons of Dried oregano
- ✓ 2 Finely grated lemons, rind

- ✓ 1 Pound of Cherry tomatoes 200 g 500 g 1 kg
- ✓ Olive oil cooking spray
- ✓ Cos lettuce leaves, shredded 4 10 20
- ✓ Lebanese cucumbers, halved, chopped

DIRECTIONS:

- ➤ Preheat your barbecue on a medium-high and a fan forced oven to
- ➤ A temperature of about 400°F
- ➤ Thread the lamb on skewers; then place in a shallow ceramic platter
- ➤ Combine all together the garlic with the oregano, the lemon and half a lemon juice in a bow
- ➤ Then season with the freshly ground pepper
- ➤ Pour the mixture over the lamb skewers and turn to coat very well
- ➤ Cover the skewers and leave in the refrigerator for about 15 minutes
- ➤ Put the tomatoes into an oven tray
- ➤ Spray with the oil, the salt and the ground pepper

- ➤ Thread the lamb onto skewers abut 4, 10 or 20 to your liking
- ➤ Put the tomatoes in an oven tray and lightly spray with oil; then season with salt and pepper
- ➤ Roast the tomatoes for about 8 minutes
- ➤ Remove the lamb from the refrigerator and barbecue on a hot BBQ for about 2 to 3 minutes per side
- ➤ Makw sure to baste with the marinade
- ➤ Combine the lettuce with the cucumber and the remaining lemon juice into a bowl
- ➤ Then toss very well to combine
- ➤ Serve and enjoy with the roasted tomatoes!

22 CHICKEN KEBABS

Servings: 6   **Cook Time: 10 Min**   **Prep Time 10 Min**

INGREDIENTS:

- ✓ 1 Chicken breast with the skin removed
- ✓ 1 Medium green pepper
- ✓ ¼ Green capsicum
- ✓ ¼ Onion
- ✓ Slices of fresh pineapple
- ✓ 2 Tablespoons of olive oil
- ✓ 3 Tablespoons of barbecue sauce
- ✓ 10 Bamboo skewers

DIRECTIONS:

- ➤ Start by soaking the bamboos skewers into water for about 1 hour before using it
- ➤ Cut the chicken into pieces
- ➤ Then wash the capsicum and pat dry with clean paper towels
- ➤ Remove the seeds from the capsicums; then cut into small squares
- ➤ Peel the onion; then chop it into quarters; then separate the onion into small segments
- ➤ Cut the pineapple into pieces of small size; then thread the chicken

- ➤ At this point onion, the pineapple and the capsicum onto bamboo skewers
- ➤ Heat the barbecue to medium high heat; then lightly brush the hot plate with oil
- ➤ Lightly brush with the barbecue sauce.
- ➤ Barbecue for about 10 minutes; make sure to turn the chicken from time to time
- ➤ Add the mushrooms, the zucchini or the cherry tomatoes
- ➤ Serve and enjoy your dish!

23 SHISH TAOUK CHICKEN

Servings: 6   **Cook Time: 10 Min**   **Prep Time 10 Min**

INGREDIENTS:

- ✓ 2 Pounds of Chicken Breast (Cut Into pieces of 2 Inch each)
- ✓ 2 Cut into chunks
- ✓ A large Green Bell Pepper with the seeds Removed
- ✓ 60ml of Fresh Lemon Juice
- ✓ 60ml of Vegetable
- ✓ Oil 180ml of Plain Yogurt
- ✓ 4 Minced garlic cloves
- ✓ 2 Teaspoons of Tomato Paste
- ✓ 1 ½ Teaspoons of Salt
- ✓ 1 Teaspoon of Dried Oregano
- ✓ ¼ Teaspoon of Ground Black Pepper
- ✓ ¼ Teaspoon of Ground All Spice
- ✓ ¼ Teaspoon of Ground Cinnamon
- ✓ ¼ Teaspoon of Ground Cardamom
- ✓ Freshly Chopped Flat Leaf Parsley

DIRECTIONS:

- ➤ In a bowl; mix altogether the lemon juice with the oil, the yogurt, the garlic
- ➤ Add the tomato paste, the oregano, the all spice, the cinnamon, the oregano, the pepper and the salt
- ➤ Then the chicken too the bag and mix very well until your chicken pieces are very well coated
- ➤ Transfer the chicken to a large plastic bag
- ➤ Then place into the refrigerator for about 4 hours
- ➤ Thread the chicken, the onion and the bell pepper onto skewers
- ➤ At this point start your barbecue and heat for about 5 minutes
- ➤ Cook the chicken for about 5 minutes per side
- ➤ Remove the kebabs from the heat; then sprinkle over some of the flat parsley
- ➤ Serve and enjoy your chicken shish taouk!

24 BARBECUED TANGY CHICKEN WINGS

Servings: 6   **Cook Time: 30 Min**   **Prep Time 10 Min**

INGREDIENTS:

- ✓ 3 Pounds of Chicken Wings A jar of
- ✓ 350ml of Peach Jam
- ✓ 240ml of Thai Sweet Red Chili Sauce
- ✓ 1 Teaspoon of Fresh Lime Juice
- ✓ 1 Tablespoon of minced Fresh Cilantro

DIRECTIONS:

- ➤ In a medium bowl, mix all together the peach jam with the lime juice, the chili sauce and the cilantro
- ➤ Pour half of the mixture into a bowl the lime juice
- ➤ Preheat your barbecue to a medium high temperature
- ➤ Then spray thegrill with oil and grill for about 20 to 25 minutes
- ➤ Apply the remaining half of the sauce and use it to glaze the chicken
- ➤ Cook for about 3 to 5 minutes; then glaze and cook for about 3 to 5 additional minutes
- ➤ Remove from the heat; then serve and enjoy your dish!

25 SMOKED TURKEY LEGS

Servings: 4   **Cook Time: 3 H**   **Prep Time 8 Min**

INGREDIENTS:

FOR THE TURKEY

- ✓ 4 to 5 whole turkey legs
- ✓ 3 to 4 tbsp of onion powder
- ✓ 3 ½ tbsp of garlic powder
- ✓ 3 ¼ tbsp of paprika
- ✓ 1 ½ tbsp of black pepper

- ✓ 1 ½ tbsp of cumin
- ✓ 1 ½ tsp of cayenne powder
- ✓ 1 Heap cup of Range Style BBQ Sauce
- ✓ 2 Tablespoons of olive Oil

FOR THE BRINE INGREDIENTS

- ✓ 1 gallon of water
- ✓ 1 Heap cup of kosher salt
- ✓ 1/2 cup of brown sugar
- ✓ 2 ¼ tbsp of garlic powder

- ✓ 2 ¼ tbsp of onion powder
- ✓ 2 ¼ tbsp of peppercorns
- ✓ 1 ¼ tbsp of paprika

DIRECTIONS:

- ➢ Combine the ingredients of the brine; then let boil and once boiling, cool down to the room temperature
- ➢ Rinse the turkey legs; then submerge into the cooled brine, you can add ice if needed
- ➢ Let the turkey brine for about 4 to 24 hours
- ➢ When the legs are completely brined; remove the turkey legs and rinse
- ➢ Then pat dry and lather with olive oil;
- ➢ Season the turkey meat with the garlic powder, the onion powder

- ➢ Add the paprika, the black pepper, the cayenne powder and the cumin
- ➢ Create a fire in your smoker with wood chips; then bring to heat of about 300°F
- ➢ Add the turkey; then let cook for about 3 hours
- ➢ At this point pull off the and baste with the range style BBQ sauce
- ➢ Smoke back for about 10 minutes
- ➢ Remove the meat from the smoker and let rest for about 10 minutes
- ➢ Serve and enjoy your dish!

26 BBQ TURKEY BREAST

Servings: 5   **Cook Time: 20 Min**   **Prep Time 10 Min**

INGREDIENTS:

FOR THE TURKEY:

- ✓ 2 lbs of turkey breast

FOR THE BBQ SAUCE :

- ✓ Use your favourite BBQ sauce

FOR THE BROWN SUGAR RUB:

- ✓ ¼ tsp of salt
- ✓ 3 tbsp of brown sugar
- ✓ 2 to 3 tbsp of chili powder

- ✓ 1 pinch of fresh ground pepper
- ✓ 2 to 3 racks of back ribs

DIRECTIONS:

- ➢ For the brown sugar rub; combine the salt with the brown sugar
- ➢ Add the chilli powder and the fresh ground pepper in a bowl
- ➢ Then prepare the turkey breast
- ➢ Separate the turkey fillet from your turkey breast and generously rub it with the salt and the pepper
- ➢ Generously rub with the rub; then preheat your BBQ to a high temperature
- ➢ Turn down the heat to low/medium

- ➢ Preheat your BBQ to high, then, turn down the heat to low/medium.
- ➢ Add the turkey and the roast to the heat and barbecue for about 20 minutes
- ➢ Make sure to coat the top of the turkey breast with your favourite BBQ sauce in the last few minutes
- ➢ Remove the turkey from the heat; then let rest for 5 minutes
- ➢ Cut the turkey into slices of about ¾ inch each
- ➢ Serve and enjoy your dish!

27 WHOLE BARBECUED TURKEY

Servings: 5   **Cook Time: 4 H**   **Prep Time 15 Min**

INGREDIENTS:

- ✓ 1 Whole turkey of about 12 pounds
- ✓ ½ cup of melted butter
- ✓ 2 tablespoons of Worcestershire sauce
- ✓ 2 tablespoons of steak sauce
- ✓ 1 tablespoon of garlic powder
- ✓ 1 tablespoon of onion powder
- ✓ 1 tablespoon of lemon-pepper seasoning
- ✓ 1 tablespoon of pepper
- ✓ 2 to 3 teaspoons of cayenne pepper
- ✓ ¼ teaspoon of salt
- ✓ 1 cup of chicken broth
- ✓ 12 split sandwich rolls
- ✓ Sliced lettuce and tomato leaves

DIRECTIONS:

- ➢ Place the turkey breast with the side up, in a large rack into a roasting pan.
- ➢ Combine all together the butter with the Worcestershire sauce, the steak sauce and the seasonings; the rub 3 tablespoons on top off the turkey.
- ➢ Cover and let refrigerate the remaining mixture of the butter
- ➢ Bake the turkey, uncovered, at a temperature of about 325° for about 3 to 3- 1/2 hours with the pan drippings
- ➢ Remove the turkey
- ➢ Then pour the drippings into a large saucepan and when turkey is cool to handle it
- ➢ Remove the meat from the bones; then return to the roasting pan
- ➢ Add in the broth and the remaining butter mixture to the drippings and bring to a rolling boil
- ➢ Pour over the shredded turkey; then turkey and return to the roasting pan and cover
- ➢ Bake at a about 325°F for about 25 to 30 minutes
- ➢ Serve and enjoy your dish

28 GRILLED FISH KEBABS

Servings: 4   **Cook Time: 10 Min**   **Prep Time 15 Min**

INGREDIENTS:

- ✓ 1 Pound of White Fish Fillets Cut Into Small Chunks
- ✓ ½ Medium Chopped Red Onion Chopped
- ✓ 80ml Olive Oil
- ✓ 2 Tablespoons of chopped Fresh cilantro
- ✓ 3 Tablespoons of Fresh Lemon Juice
- ✓ ½ Teaspoon of Paprika
- ✓ ½ Teaspoon of Salt
- ✓ ¼ Teaspoon of Freshly
- ✓ Ground Black Pepper
- ✓ ¼ Teaspoon of Chilli Powder
- ✓ 2 Minced Garlic Cloves
- ✓ Wooden skewers

DIRECTIONS:

- ➢ Start by cutting the fillets of the fish into chunks; then place in a resealable plastic bag
- ➢ Place the onion, the olive oil, the cilantro, the lemon juice, the paprika
- ➢ Add the salt, the pepper, the chilli powder and the minced garlic
- ➢ Stir very well to make sure that your ingredients are very well mixed
- ➢ Close the prepared bag and turn it several times to shake very well
- ➢ Place the ingredients into the bag in your refrigerator and leave for about 2 to 4 hours
- ➢ When the barbecuing time comes; remove the fish from the bag and there for between 2 and 4 hours.
- ➢ Thread each skewer with the fish
- ➢ Make sure to oil the grill on your preheated barbecue; then place the skewers on it
- ➢ Cook the fish kebabs on a medium high heat for about 8 to 10 minutes
- ➢ Remove the fish from the barbecue; then serve and enjoy with a salad of your choice!

29 AMERICA'S BEST BARBEQUE RUB

Servings: 8 **Cook Time: 10 Min** **Prep Time 10 Min**

INGREDIENTS:

- ✓ 1/4 cup firmly packed brown sugar
- ✓ 1/4 cup sweet paprika
- ✓ 3 tbsps. ground black pepper
- ✓ 3 tbsps. coarse salt
- ✓ 2 tbsps. ground cumin
- ✓ 1 tbsp. hickory smoked salt
- ✓ 2 tsps. garlic powder
- ✓ 2 tsps. onion powder
- ✓ 2 tsps. celery seeds
- ✓ 1 tsp. cayenne pepper

DIRECTIONS:

- ➤ Mix cayenne pepper, celery seeds, onion powder, garlic powder
- ➤ Add hickory salt, cumin, coarse salt, black pepper, paprika, and brown sugar together in a bowl.

30 ASIAN FIESTA CHICKEN MARINADE

Servings: 4 **Cook Time: 0 Min** **Prep Time 2 H**

INGREDIENTS:

- ✓ 1/3 cup Kikkoman Soy Sauce
- ✓ 1 lemon, juiced
- ✓ 2 cloves garlic, minced
- ✓ 1/4 cup fresh cilantro
- ✓ 1/2 cup olive oil
- ✓ 1 tsp. onion powder
- ✓ 1/2 tsp. coarsely ground black pepper
- ✓ 2 lbs. boneless, skinless chicken breasts

DIRECTIONS:

- ➤ Mix black pepper, onion powder, olive oil, cilantro, garlic, lemon juice and Kikkoman Soy Sauce well.
- ➤ Into the refrigerator, add chicken into the marinade, and marinate for no less than 2 hours or overnight
- ➤ Grill as your favorite way. Serve alongside your favorite salsa.

31 AWESOME STEAK MARINADE

Servings: 2 **Cook Time: 5 Min** **Prep Time 5 Min**

INGREDIENTS:

- ✓ 1 1/2 cups steak sauce
- ✓ 1 tbsp. soy sauce
- ✓ 1/3 cup Italian-style salad dressing
- ✓ 1/3 cup honey
- ✓ 1/2 tsp. garlic powder

DIRECTIONS:

- ➤ Blend garlic powder, honey, Italian-style dressing, soy sauce
- ➤ Steak sauce for 10 seconds in a blender
- ➤ Put on any kind of steak then cover
- ➤ Sit overnight, occasionally turning to coat all the sides.

32 BACKYARD BOURBON BEEF MARINADE

Servings: 6 **Cook Time: 0 Min** **Prep Time 5 Min**

INGREDIENTS:

- ✓ 1 cup Kikkoman Soy Sauce
- ✓ 3/4 cup water
- ✓ 3 tbsps. bourbon
- ✓ 2 tbsps. sugar
- ✓ 1 tsp. crushed garlic clove
- ✓ 1 tbsp. confectioners' sugar
- ✓ 2 lbs. beef flank steak

DIRECTIONS:

- ➤ Combine all ingredients excluding the beef flank steak, and marinate meat in the refrigerator for 12 to 24 hours
- ➤ Grill using preferred method.

33 BANGIN' STEAK RUB

Servings: 10   **Cook Time: 0 Min**   **Prep Time 5 Min**

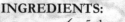

INGREDIENTS:

- ✓ 1/2 cup packed brown sugar
- ✓ 1 (1.25 oz.) package chili seasoning mix
- ✓ 1 (1 oz.) envelope ranch dressing mix
- ✓ 1 tsp. garlic salt
- ✓ 1 tsp. onion salt
- ✓ 1/2 tsp. ground black pepper
- ✓ 1 tsp. steak seasoning

DIRECTIONS:

- ➢ Totally combine steak seasoning, ground black pepper, onion salt, garlic salt, ranch dressing mix
- ➢ Add chili seasoning mix and brown sugar in small-sized bowl
- ➢ The rub should be in smooth and granular texture, with no big lumps remains
- ➢ Keep it rest at room temperature in an airtight container till ready to use.
- ➢ To use, rub the seasoning mix freely onto the meat or steak that you want prior to cooking.

34 BAYOU'S BODACIOUS PORK RUB

Servings: 168   **Cook Time: 0 Min**   **Prep Time 15 Min**

INGREDIENTS:

- ✓ 5 tbsps. kosher salt
- ✓ 6 tbsps. paprika
- ✓ 10 tbsps. dark brown sugar
- ✓ 3 tbsps. file powder (powdered sassafras leaves)
- ✓ 2 tbsps. ground dried thyme
- ✓ 2 tbsps. dried dill weed
- ✓ 2 tbsps. dried oregano
- ✓ 2 tbsps. dried basil
- ✓ 2 tbsps. ground black pepper
- ✓ 10 tbsps. garlic powder
- ✓ 10 tbsps. onion powder
- ✓ 1 tbsp. cayenne pepper
- ✓ 2 tbsps. dry mustard powder
- ✓ 2 tbsps. ground allspice
- ✓ 2 tbsps. ground dried sage

DIRECTIONS:

- ➢ In a bowl, mix sage, allspice, mustard, cayenne pepper, onion powder, garlic powder, black pepper
- ➢ Add basil, oregano, dill, thyme, file powder, brown sugar, paprika and salt till blended equally
- ➢ Keep the rub rest at room temperature in an airtight container.
- ➢ To use: freely coat brisket or pork butt with some of the rub, massaging the rub to the meat
- ➢ Use plastic wrap to wrap the meat tightly
- ➢ Keep in the refrigerator for no less than 1 day
- ➢ Smoke meat the way you usually do.

35 BBQ SPICE RUB

Servings: 8 **Cook Time: 0 Min** **Prep Time 5 Min**

INGREDIENTS:
- ✓ 1/2 cup brown sugar
- ✓ 1/2 cup paprika
- ✓ 1 tbsp. ground black pepper
- ✓ 1 tbsp. salt
- ✓ 1 tbsp. chili powder
- ✓ 1 tbsp. garlic powder
- ✓ 1 tbsp. onion powder
- ✓ 1 tsp. cayenne pepper (optional)

DIRECTIONS:
- ➢ In a bowl, stir cayenne pepper, onion powder, garlic powder, chili powder, salt, black pepper, paprika, and brown sugar
- ➢ Keep in a plastic bag that is sealable in the freezer or in an airtight container.

36 BEEF FAJITA MARINADE

Servings: 4 **Cook Time: 0 Min** **Prep Time 15 Min**

INGREDIENTS:
- ✓ 1/3 cup fresh lime juice
- ✓ 1/4 cup tequila
- ✓ 2 cloves garlic, minced
- ✓ 1 tbsp. chopped cilantro
- ✓ 1 tsp. dried, crushed Mexican oregano
- ✓ 2 tsps. ground cumin
- ✓ 1 tsp. freshly ground black pepper

DIRECTIONS:
- ➢ Whisk pepper, cumin, oregano, cilantro, garlic, tequila and lime juice in bowl.
- ➢ Use marinade: Put in resealable bag; add 1-1 1/2-lb. flank steak
- ➢ Press air out of bag; tightly seal. Marinade for 8-24 hours in the fridge.

37 BEEF OR CHICKEN MARINADE

Servings: 12 **Marinate: 4 H** **Prep Time 10 Min**

INGREDIENTS:
- ✓ 1/4 cup soy sauce
- ✓ 3 tbsps. honey
- ✓ 2 tbsps. distilled white vinegar
- ✓ 1 1/2 tsps. garlic powder
- ✓ 1 1/2 tsps. ground ginger
- ✓ 3/4 cup vegetable oil
- ✓ 2 green onions, chopped
- ✓ 1 tsp. coarsely ground black pepper

DIRECTIONS:
- ➢ Mix black pepper, green onions, vegetable oil, ground ginger, garlic powder
- ➢ Add distilled white vinegar, honey and soy sauce in big bowl
- ➢ In marinade, put desired mea
- ➢ Marinate for 4 hours at least before grilling in the fridge.

38 QUICK SMOKED KING FISH

Servings: 4 **Cook Time 1 H** **Prep Time 20 Min**

INGREDIENTS:

- ✓ 8 cups of water
- ✓ 7 ounces of dark brown sugar
- ✓ 14 ounces of salt
- ✓ About 2 to 3 pounds of kingfish fillets

DIRECTIONS:

- ➤ First of all, please assemble all the ingredients at one place
- ➤ Whisk the water with brown sugar & salt in a large bowl or pot and soak in it the fillet
- ➤ Then let them soak for few hours.
- ➤ Now preheat the smoker on 340 to 350 F.
- ➤ One thing remains to be done.
- ➤ At this point drain the fish fillets from the brine & smoke them for about 45 to 50 min.
- ➤ Finally once the time is up
- ➤ Cover the fish with a piece of foil & allow them to rest for about 5 to 12 min then serve it & enjoy.

39 WONDERFUL FIVE SPICE PORK ASADO

Servings: 4 **Cook Time : 30 Min** **Prep Time 20 Min**

INGREDIENTS:

- ✓ 1 teaspoon garlic (Minced)
- ✓ 1 to 2 cups water
- ✓ 11/2 lbs pork
- ✓ 1/3 cup brown sugar
- ✓ About 2.5 tablespoons rice wine
- ✓ 1/4 teaspoon salt
- ✓ 1 cup soy sauce
- ✓ About 1.5 teaspoon five spice powder

DIRECTIONS:

- ➤ First of all, please assemble all the ingredients at one place
- ➤ Cut the pork into bite size pieces.
- ➤ Then in a bowl combine the minced garlic, soy sauce, rice wine, salt, brown sugar, water & five spice.
- ➤ Mix well and add to a pot.
- ➤ This step is important. Heat over medium high heat & let it thickened.
- ➤ Now season the pork using salt & some five spice.
- ➤ One thing remains to be done
- ➤ Grill for about 2 to 5 minutes on each side.
- ➤ Finally serve the pork with the five spice sauce.

40 ELEGANT SPICY AND SWEET JALAPENO BBQ SAUCE

Servings: 2   **Cook Time: 45 Min**   **Prep Time 5 Min**

INGREDIENTS:
- ✓ 1/2 cup brown sugar, packed
- ✓ 1/2 teaspoon ground cayenne pepper
- ✓ 1 whole jalapeno, grilled for about 2 minutes
- ✓ About 1.5 teaspoon cumin
- ✓ 15 ounces tomato sauce, canned
- ✓ 1/2 cup apple cider vinegar
- ✓ 1 tablespoon Worcestershire sauce
- ✓ 1 teaspoon ground mustard
- ✓ About 1.5 tablespoon onion powder
- ✓ 1 tablespoon garlic powder
- ✓ 1 teaspoon salt
- ✓ 1/2 cup butter, unsalted

DIRECTIONS:
- ➢ First of all, please assemble all the ingredients at one place
- ➢ Place the butter in a saucepan.
- ➢ Then please set the pan on the stove over medium heat & melt the Stir in the brown sugar
- ➢ Bring to a boil, & boil for about 5 to 10 minutes.
- ➢ Place the grilled jalapeno pepper into a blender.
- ➢ This step is important
- ➢ Add the tomato sauce & blend until there are no chunks left.

- ➢ One thing remains to be done
- ➢ Use the sauce immediately or transfer to a mason jar.
- ➢ Now transfer the tomato mixture into the butter mixture.
- ➢ Add the Worcestershire sauce, vinegar, onion powder, ground mustard, cumin, salt, cayenne pepper, & garlic powder.
- ➢ Stir until well combined.
- ➢ Then let the mixture simmer for about 30 to 35 minutes, making sure to stir the mixture frequently.
- ➢ Next, please remove the sauce from the heat & let it cool down a bit.
- ➢ Finally store unused BBQ sauce in the fridge for up to 7 to 10 days.

41 AWESOME BUTTERFLIED TROUT

Servings: 8   **Cook Time: 9 H**   **Prep Time 25 Min**

INGREDIENTS:
- ✓ About 1.5 tablespoon of Black pepper
- ✓ 1/2 gallon of water
- ✓ 1/2 cup of brown sugar
- ✓ About 1.5 cup of salt
- ✓ 4 whole rainbow trout, cleaned and butterflied

DIRECTIONS:
- ➢ First of all, please assemble all the ingredients at one place
- ➢ Preheat the smoker on 390 to 400 F.
- ➢ Now whisk the sugar with water & salt in a large bowl to make the brine
- ➢ Then place in it the trout and refrigerate them for 2 h.
- ➢ One thing remains to be done
- ➢ At this point drain the fish
- ➢ Place it in the smoker with the skin facing down then smoke it for about 15 to 20 min.
- ➢ Finally once the time is up, serve your smoke trout warm & enjoy.

42 SUPER SIMPLE CHICKEN ASADO

Servings: 8   **Cook Time: 30 Min**   **Prep Time 1 H 30 Min**

INGREDIENTS:

- ✓ 1/4 cup lemon juice
- ✓ 3/4 cup cooking oil
- ✓ 2 tablespoons soy sauce
- ✓ About 1 teaspoon ground black pepper
- ✓ 1/4 cup butter
- ✓ 11/2 cup of tomato sauce
- ✓ About 1 teaspoon salt
- ✓ 4 large onion (Diced)
- ✓ 2 large potatoes, quartered
- ✓ 2 lbs chicken, cut into serving pieces

DIRECTIONS:

- ➢ First of all, please assemble all the ingredients at one place
- ➢ In a medium mixing bowl please combine the lemon juice, butter, soy sauce, tomato sauce, salt and pepper.
- ➢ Now mix well and add the chicken, onion & potatoes.
- ➢ This step is important. Coat well & set aside for 1 hour.
- ➢ Next, please grill the chicken for about 5 to 10 minutes on each side.
- ➢ One thing remains to be done
- ➢ Then grill the potatoes for about 5 to 10 minutes & the onion for about 2 to 5 minutes.
- ➢ Finally serve all of them together.

43 ENERGETIC SMOKED STEELHEAD TROUT

Servings: 8   **Cook Time: 6 H**   **Prep Time 30 Min**

INGREDIENTS:

- ✓ 1 cup of brown sugar
- ✓ 1 clove of garlic, finely chopped
- ✓ 1/2 cup of kosher salt
- ✓ About 1.5 teaspoon of ground ginger
- ✓ About 1.5 teaspoon of white pepper
- ✓ 5 pounds of steelhead trout fillets

DIRECTIONS:

- ➢ First of all, please assemble all the ingredients at one place
- ➢ Rinse the trout fillets & pat them dry then set them aside.
- ➢ Now mix the rest of the ingredients in a small bowl to make the cure.
- ➢ One thing remains to be done
- ➢ Lay a piece of a food plastic wrap & sprinkle on it half of the cure
- ➢ Then lay on it the trout fillets & sprinkle on them the rest of the cure
- ➢ Refrigerate them for 6 h to an overnight.
- ➢ At this point shake the trout fillets from the cure & place them in the smoker
- ➢ Then smoke them for 4 to 5 h or until they reach 150 F.
- ➢ Finally allow the trout fillets to rest for about 10 to 15 min then serve them & enjoy.

44 GRILLED AVOCADO CAPRESE CROSTINI

Servings: 4   **Cook Time: 20 Min**   **Prep Time 30 Min**

INGREDIENTS:

- ✓ 1 avocado, sliced thinly
- ✓ 2 tablespoons olive oil
- ✓ 1/2 cup basil leaves, divided
- ✓ 8 pieces sliced French or Italian baguette, sliced 1/2-inch thick
- ✓ 2 tablespoons balsamic glaze
- ✓ 3.5 ounces (100 grams) fresh bocconcini in water (or baby mozzarella balls)
- ✓ 9 ounces (250 grams) vine ripened cherry tomatoes, halved

DIRECTIONS:

- ➢ Heat up the oven to 375°F | 190°C.
- ➢ On a baking sheet, arrange the bread
- ➢ Sprinkle olive oil on both sides
- ➢ Now bake for about fifteen (15) twenty (20) minutes until it becomes golden
- ➢ As you bake, be toasting it by flipping so that it becomes crisp all over. While it is still warm, rub the crostini with the cut side of the garlic, use little pepper and salt to season.
- ➢ On each slice of bread, divide ¼ cup of the basil leaves, per bread, it should be about 2-3 basil leaves
- ➢ Now use the avocado slices, mozzarella (bocconcini), and tomato halves as toppings for each
- ➢ You can use pepper and/or salt as seasoning to taste.
- ➢ You should grill or broil until the cheese has began melting through, and it normally takes about three (3) to five (5) minutes.
- ➢ Finally, neatly chop the basil leaves that are remaining
- ➢ Sprinkle it over the crostini, and use balsamic glaze to drizzle it for serving.

45 SMOKEY GRILLED SWEET POTATO WEDGES

Servings: 6   **Cook Time: 12 Min**   **Prep Time 10 Min**

INGREDIENTS:

- ✓ 2 teaspoons Oil
- ✓ 2 teaspoons finely chopped Fresh Cilantro
- ✓ 1 tablespoon Homemade Southwestern Pork Rub
- ✓ 20 ounces Sweet Potatoes, washed and dried

DIRECTIONS:

- ➢ Close the lid and reheat the grill until it attains medium heat.
- ➢ Cut the sweet potatoes into large wedges without peeling off the skin
- ➢ The size of the cut potatoes should look like thick cut steak fries
- ➢ Move the sweet potatoes you just cut onto a large baking sheet
- ➢ Sprinkle oil on it, and as you do so, toss it to become evenly coat.
- ➢ You should now uniformly sprinkle part of the homemade southwestern pork (about half) over the oiled sweet potatoes
- ➢ Turn over and drizzle on the other side the remaining rub.
- ➢ Bring out the sweet potatoes from the baking sheet and immediately transfer them to the hot grill
- ➢ For about three (3) to four (4) minutes, cook, and don't forget to close the lid
- ➢ Now flip it over and cook on the other side for an extra three (3) to four (4) minutes.

Note: If it happens that the sweet potatoes are not soft enough after you have grilled both sides, move to a top rack in the grill and bring down the heat to medium-low. Then cook until it becomes tender

- ➢ Bring down the sweet potatoes from the grill, move it to the baking sheet that was initially used, and grizzle it with cilantro. Finally, serve.

Notes: It is highly recommended that you make use of Avocado Oil, Safflower, Canola, or Sunflower Oil, for grilling. This is because they have a high smoke point.

46 COCONUT PINEAPPLE SHRIMP SKEWERS

Serving: 1   Cook Time: 5 Min   Prep Time 20 Min

INGREDIENTS:
- ✓ 3/4 pound 1 inch-cut pineapple chunks
- ✓ 4 teaspoons Tabasco Original Red Sauce
- ✓ Canola oil, for grilling
- ✓ 1/4 cup freshly squeezed lime juice (from about 2 large limes)
- ✓ 2 teaspoons soy sauce
- ✓ 1 pound large (31-40 count) shrimp, peeled and deveined (you can use fresh or frozen, thawed shrimp)
- ✓ 1/2 cup light coconut milk
- ✓ Freshly chopped cilantro and/or green onion, for serving
- ✓ 1/4 cup freshly squeezed orange juice

DIRECTIONS:
- ➤ Combine these ingredients in a medium bowl: lime juice, Tabasco sauce
- ➤ Add soy sauce, orange juice, and the coconut milk
- ➤ Now, in order to coat, add the shrimp and toss
- ➤ Cover and put inside a fridge for about one (1) two (2) hours and toss from time to time to marinate
- ➤ Toss it from time to time
- ➤ (If you are making use of wooden skewers, make sure it is soaked in warm water while allowing the shrimp marinate)
- ➤ You should get the pineapple prepared if need be.
- ➤ To medium heat, preheat the grill
- ➤ Bring out the shrimp from the marinade and keep it reserved for grilling

- ➤ Now unto a skewers you should thread the shrimp, and keep alternating with the pineapple.
- ➤ Use canola oil to brush the grill lightly, then put the shrimp on top of the grill
- ➤ You should grill the shrimp for about three (3) minutes, and as you grill, use the marinade to brush it
- ➤ Then turn it and cook for an extra two (2) to three (3) minutes again, using the marinade to brush
- ➤ (Until you find the shrimp cooked thoroughly)
- ➤ Now transfer it unto a serving plate
- ➤ Make use of green onion and cilantro to garnish. Finally, serve hot!

47 TOM'S BLACKENED SEASONING

Servings: 24   Cook Time: 10 Min   Prep Time 10 Min

INGREDIENTS:
- ✓ 1 tbsp. paprika
- ✓ 4 tsps. dried thyme
- ✓ 2 tsps. onion powder
- ✓ 2 tsps. garlic powder
- ✓ 1 tbsp. white sugar
- ✓ 2 tsps. salt

- ✓ 1 1/2 tsps. black pepper
- ✓ 1 tsp. cayenne pepper, or to taste
- ✓ 1 tsp. dried oregano
- ✓ 1/2 tsp. ground nutmeg
- ✓ 3/4 tsp. ground cumin

DIRECTIONS:
- ➤ Mix cumin, nutmeg, oregano, cayenne pepper, pepper, salt, sugar
- ➤ Add garlic powder, onion powder, thyme and paprika in a small lidded jar

- ➤ Blending the mixture by sealing carefully and shaking forcefully
- ➤ Keep in cool dry place. Before each use, shake jar.

48 TRI-TIP RUB

Servings: 6 Cook Time: 25 Min Prep Time 5 Min

INGREDIENTS:
- ✓ 3 tbsps. garlic powder
- ✓ 2 tbsps. salt
- ✓ 2 tbsps. ground black pepper
- ✓ 2 lbs. tri tip roast

DIRECTIONS:
- ➤ Preheat an outdoor grill for high heat and oil the grate a bit.
- ➤ Mix pepper, salt, and garlic powder in a medium-sized bowl
- ➤ Stir together and coat the tri tip's both sides.
- ➤ Sear both sides on hot grill
- ➤ Cook till the middle part turns a bit pink in color for 20 to 25 minutes. Cut at an angle.

49 TURKEY RUB (POULTRY RUB)

Servings: 7 Cook Time: 0 Min Prep Time 10 Min

INGREDIENTS:
- ✓ 1 tbsp. dried thyme
- ✓ 1 tbsp. dried rosemary
- ✓ 1 tbsp. dried marjoram
- ✓ 1 tsp. coarse salt (such as Himalayan)
- ✓ 3 tbsps. molasses

DIRECTIONS:
- ➤ Use a mortar and pestle to crush salt, marjoram, rosemary, and thyme together
- ➤ Stir in molasses until completely incorporated

50 GRILLED ASPARAGUS RECIPE

Servings: 5 Cook Time: 10 Min Prep Time 15 Min

INGREDIENTS:
- ✓ Salt and pepper
- ✓ 3 Tablespoons grated parmesan cheese
- ✓ 1 pound fresh asparagus
- ✓ 2 Garlic Cloves, minced
- ✓ 2 Tablespoons olive oil

DIRECTIONS:
- ➤ Get the asparagus prepared and cut out the bottoms to trim it
- ➤ Place the asparagus in the pan
- ➤ Sprinkle with pepper and salt, and pour in the olive oil.
- ➤ In a row, lay the asparagus on the grill. Over medium heat, grill for about five (5) ten (10) minutes
- ➤ During this grill time, watch out till they becomes tender and also have char marks
- ➤ Bring out the asparagus and put it back into the pan
- ➤ Toss it with parmesan cheese and garlic. Finally, serve!

NOTE: if you so desire, you can use a foil to grill the asparagus.

51 SWEET HEAT CHEERWINE BABY BACK RIBS

Servings: 8   **Cook Time: 3 H**   **Prep Time 30 Min**

INGREDIENTS:
- ✓ 2 tsp. chili-garlic sauce
- ✓ 2 tsp. chili powder
- ✓ 1 (15-oz.) can tomato sauce
- ✓ 1 tsp. garlic powder
- ✓ 2 tsp. smoked paprika
- ✓ 1 tsp. ground ginger
- ✓ 1/3 c. light brown sugar
- ✓ Kosher salt and freshly ground black pepper
- ✓ 2 tsp. dry mustard
- ✓ 2 (3-lb.) slabs baby back ribs
- ✓ 1 tbsp. Dijon mustard
- ✓ 1 (12-oz.) bottle Cheerwine soft drink

DIRECTIONS:
- ➤ To 325°F, preheat the oven.
- ➤ Together in a bowl, stir the dry mustard, 2 teaspoons pepper, paprika, garlic powder
- ➤ Add 4 teaspoons salt, chili powder, and ginger
- ➤ Get two (2) tablespoons of spice mixture and sprinkle over ribs, dividing equally
- ➤ On a rimmed baking sheet, place the ribs, and use aluminum foil to wrap tightly
- ➤ Bake for about two (2) to two and half (2 ½) hours till it becomes tender
- ➤ Remove the foil and keep it to rest for about thirty minutes.
- ➤ Get a medium saucepan and mix together the Dijon mustard,

- ➤ tomato sauce, 1 tablespoon spice mixture, brown sugar, chili-garlic sauce, and Cheerwine
- ➤ Now over high heat, bring to a boil
- ➤ Turn down the heat and simmer
- ➤ As you do so, keep stirring it from time to time for about twety five (25) to thirty (30) minutes
- ➤ (Until it gets reduced to two (2) cups)
- ➤ To medium level, heat the grill, now grill ribs
- ➤ As you grill, be basting with a cup of the cheerwine sauce, and keep turning regularly
- ➤ It should take about ten (10) to fifteen (15) minutes, when it will become lacquered and lightly charred.
- ➤ Finally, transfer unto a serving dish and serve with the spice mixture and cheerwine that is remaining.

52 BARBECUED SHRIMP

Servings: 3   **Cook Time: 10 Min**   **Prep Time 5 Min**

INGREDIENTS:
- ✓ ¼ Cup of extra-virgin olive oil
- ✓ ¼ Cup of lime juice
- ✓ 4 Minced garlic cloves
- ✓ 3 tbsp of honey
- ✓ 2 tbsp of low-sodium soy sauce
- ✓ 1 tbsp of chili garlic sauce or of Sriracha
- ✓ 2 lb of peeled and dveined shrimp
- ✓ ¼ Cup of freshly chopped cilantro, for garnish
- ✓ Lime wedges, for serving

DIRECTIONS:
- ➤ In a medium bowl, whisk all together the olive oil with the lime juice, the garlic
- ➤ Add the honey, the soy sauce, and the chili sauce.
- ➤ Reserve about ¼ cup of the marinade for brushing it onto the shrimp while grilling.
- ➤ In a large bowl, toss the shrimp with the remaining marinade.

- ➤ Preheat your Barbecue
- ➤ Then thread the shrimp into skewers
- ➤ Grill for about 3 minutes per side making
- ➤ Sure to brush with the reserved ¼ cup of the marinade before and after each flip
- ➤ Garnish with the cilantro; then serve and enjoy hot with the lime wedges.

53 CHARMING TIRA BARBECUED SHORT RIBS , TOMATILLO SALSA

Servings: 6   **Cook Time: 20 Min**   **Prep Time 1 H**

INGREDIENTS:

- ✓ Sea salt to taste
- ✓ 1 onion (Diced)
- ✓ Black pepper to taste
- ✓ About 2.5 tablespoon vinegar 1
- ✓ /2 cup herbs
- ✓ Tomatillo Salsa

- ✓ 1 lb tomatillos
- ✓ About 1.5 tablespoon lime juice
- ✓ 3 cloves garlic (Minced)
- ✓ 1/2 jalapeno (Diced)
- ✓ lb beef short ribs, cut into slices
- ✓ Salt to taste

DIRECTIONS:

- ➢ First of all, please assemble all the ingredients at one place
- ➢ Season the beef using salt & pepper.
- ➢ Now run the beef slices using vinegar & let it marinate for about 1.5 hour.

- ➢ Build a charcoal fire & add the beef to the fire.
- ➢ Then char for about 5 to 10 minutes on each side.
- ➢ One thing remains to be done
- ➢ Combine the tomatillo salsa Ingredients in a bowl.
- ➢ Finally mix well & serve with the charcoaled beef.

54 BARBECUE WHITE FISH

Servings: 4   **Cook Time: 10 Min**   **Prep Time 5 Min**

INGREDIENTS:

- ✓ 1 tsp of chili powder
- ✓ 1 tsp of dried oregano
- ✓ ¼ tsp of cayenne pepper
- ✓ 1 Pinch of Kosher salt

- ✓ 1 Pinch of Freshly ground black pepper
- ✓ 1 White fish, like bass or cod of about 1 ½ inches of thickness
- ✓ Lime wedges, for serving

DIRECTIONS:

- ➢ Heat your barbecue to high heat
- ➢ Whisk all together the chilli powder with the oregano, the cayenne
- ➢ Season with 1 pinch of salt and 1 pinch of pepper
- ➢ Season the fish with the mixture of the spices

- ➢ Cook with the skin side down for about 8 to 10 minutes
- ➢ Flip and cook for 2 to 3 additional minutes
- ➢ Serve and enjoy your dish!

54 BBQ SALAD

Servings: 4   **Cook Time: 10 Min**   **Prep Time 16 Min**

INGREDIENTS:

- ✓ 2 tbsp extra virgin olive oil
- ✓ 1 tbsp lemon juice
- ✓ 1 small garlic clove, minced
- ✓ 1/2 tsp Dijon mustard
- ✓ 1/8 tsp Worcestershire sauce
- ✓ 1/4 tsp black pepper
- ✓ 2 tbsp grated parmesan cheese olive oil flavored cooking spray
- ✓ 2 romaine lettuce hearts

DIRECTIONS:

- ➢ Get a mixing bowl: Mix in it the oil, lemon juice, garlic, mustard, Worcestershire, and pepper.
- ➢ Add the parmesan cheese and combine them well to make the dressing.
- ➢ Place it in the fridge until ready to serve.
- ➢ Before you do anything, preheat the grill and grease it.

- ➢ Slice the romaine hearts in half lengthwise. Coat them with a cooking spray.
- ➢ Grill them for 3 to 4 min on each side. Serve them warm with the cheese dressing.
- ➢ Enjoy.

55 TATER TOTS ON THE BBQ

Servings: 6   Cook Time: 32 Min   Prep Time 40 Min

INGREDIENTS:

- ✓ Spice Mix
- ✓ 1 C. salt
- ✓ 1/4 C. black pepper
- ✓ 1/4 C. garlic powder
- ✓ Potatoes
- ✓ 3 golden delight potatoes, sliced into coins
- ✓ 1/4 large sweet onion, sliced
- ✓ 1 1/2 tbsp salted butter, melted
- ✓ House seasoning

DIRECTIONS:

- ➢ Before you do anything, preheat the grill and grease it.
- ➢ Get a large piece of oil. Fold it in half.
- ➢ Divide between them the potatoes, onion, salt, pepper, garlic powder and melted butter on top.
- ➢ Cover them with a piece of foil. Pinch the edges and seal them.
- ➢ Place it on the grill. Put on the lid and let it cook for 16 to 20 min.
- ➢ Once the time is up, remove the lid and let it cook for an extra 10 to 12 min. Serve it warm.
- ➢ Enjoy.

56 AFRICAN RUMP STEAK

Servings: 8   Cook Time: 10 Min   Prep Time 8 Min

INGREDIENTS:

- ✓ 2 1/2 lbs. rump steak
- ✓ 1/2 C. chutney
- ✓ 1/2 C. ketchup
- ✓ 1/4 C. Worcestershire sauce
- ✓ 1 tbsp white vinegar
- ✓ 3 tbsp apple cider vinegar
- ✓ 2 garlic cloves, minced
- ✓ 2 onions, sliced
- ✓ 1 (8 oz.) cans mushrooms, drained salt and pepper

DIRECTIONS:

- ➢ Slice the steak into large chunks. Sprinkle over them some salt and pepper.
- ➢ Get a mixing bowl: Whisk in it the remaining ingredients.
- ➢ Add the steak chunks and toss them to coat. Cover it and let it sit for 60 min.
- ➢ Before you do anything, preheat the grill and grease it.
- ➢ Drain the steaks pieces and grill them for 6 to 10 min on each side. Serve them warm.
- ➢ Enjoy.

57 MENDOZA KABOBS

Servings: 4   Cook Time: 30 Min   Prep Time 15 Min

INGREDIENTS:

- ✓ 4 chicken breasts, diced
- ✓ 1/2 red bell pepper, cut into squares
- ✓ 1/2 green bell pepper, cut into squares
- ✓ 2 yellow onions, cut into eighths
- ✓ 1 C. cherry tomatoes bamboo skewer
- ✓ 1/2 C. oil
- ✓ 3 cloves garlic, chopped
- ✓ 1 tsp paprika
- ✓ 1/2 tsp Mexican oregano kosher salt
- ✓ Black peppercorns

DIRECTIONS:

- ➢ Before you do anything, preheat the grill and grease it.
- ➢ Get a food processor: Combine in it the Oil, Garlic, Paprika, Oregano, Salt, and Peppercorns.
- ➢ Process them several times until they become smooth to make the marinade.
- ➢ Get a large mixing bowl: Combine in it the chicken dices with marinade.
- ➢ Cover the bowl and let it sit for at least 20 min.
- ➢ Before you do anything else, preheat the grill and grease it.
- ➢ Thread the chicken dices with onion, peppers, and cherry tomatoes onto skewers while alternating between them.
- ➢ Grill them for 8 to 10 min on each side. Serve them warm.
- ➢ Enjoy.

58 CREOLE FISH

Servings: 8   **Cook Time: 15 Min**   **Prep Time 10 Min**

INGREDIENTS:

- ✓ Vegetables
- ✓ 1/4 c. Olive oil
- ✓ 4 cloves roasted garlic, minced
- ✓ 1 red pepper, quartered
- ✓ 1 portabella mushroom
- ✓ 1 onion, sliced
- ✓ 1 zucchini, sliced into
- ✓ 4 long strips 3 tbsp olive oil
- ✓ 3 tbsp balsamic vinegar tsp italian seasoning dressing

- ✓ 2 cloves garlic, minced
- ✓ Directions
- ✓ 1/8 c. Balsamic vinegar
- ✓ 1 sprig rosemary, stem discarded leaves chopped
- ✓ Salad
- ✓ 16 oz. Cheese tortellini
- ✓ 1/2 c. Provolone cheese, diced 4 oz. Black olives
- ✓ Salt and pepper

DIRECTIONS:

- ➤ Get a large zip lock bag: Combine in it the veggies with oil, vinegar, and Italian seasoning.
- ➤ Seal the bag and let them sit for 60 min in the fridge.
- ➤ Before you do anything, preheat the grill and grease it.
- ➤ Grill the veggies for 3 to 4 min on each side.
- ➤ Place them aside to cool down for a bit. Dice them.

- ➤ Get a food processor: Combine in it the salad dressing ingredients. Blend them smooth.
- ➤ Get a large mixing bowl: Combine in it the grilled veggies with tortellini, cheese, olives, dressing, a pinch of salt and pepper.
- ➤ Stir them to coat. Adjust the seasoning of your salad then serve it with extra toppings of your choice.
- ➤ Enjoy

59 TEXAS SIRLOINS

Servings: 8   **Cook Time: 15 Min**   **Prep Time 24 H 5 Min**

INGREDIENTS:

- ✓ 1 1/2 lbs. top sirloin steaks
- ✓ 2 tbsp vegetable oil
- ✓ 1 tsp dried oregano leaves
- ✓ 1 tsp garlic powder
- ✓ 1/2 tsp salt
- ✓ 1 tsp ground pepper
- ✓ 1/4 C. orange juice
- ✓ 2 tsp cider vinegar

DIRECTIONS:

- ➤ Get a mixing bowl: Toss in it all the ingredients.
- ➤ Cover the bowl and let it sit overnight.
- ➤ Before you do anything, preheat the grill and grease it.
- ➤ Drain the steaks and grill them for 10 to 14 min on each side. Serve them warm.
- ➤ Enjoy.

60 MIAMI CAFFE' SCALLOPS

Servings: 2 **Cook Time: 10 Min** **Prep Time 5 Min**

INGREDIENTS:

- ✓ 12 oz. frozen sea scallops, thawed and drained
- ✓ 1 tsp dried thyme
- ✓ 1 tsp ground black pepper
- ✓ 1 tsp kosher salt
- ✓ 1 tsp lime zest

DIRECTIONS:

- ➤ Soak the bamboo skewers in water for 10 to 20 min.
- ➤ Drain them and thread onto them the scallops.
- ➤ Get a mixing bowl: Mix in it the rest of the ingredients
- ➤ Massage the mixture gently into the scallops.
- ➤ Before you do anything, preheat the grill and grease it.
- ➤ Grill the scallop skewers for 2 to 4 min on each side. Serve them warm.
- ➤ Enjoy.

61 SOUTHWEST RIB-EYE STEAKS

Servings: 6 **Cook Time: 2 H 15 Min** **Prep Time 10 Min**

INGREDIENTS:

- ✓ 4 oz. bunch flat leaf parsley, stemmed, chopped
- ✓ 4 oz. bunch cilantro, chopped
- ✓ 3 garlic cloves, minced
- ✓ 2 tbsp ground cumin
- ✓ 1 tbsp ground coriander
- ✓ 2 tbsp sweet paprika
- ✓ 1 tsp smoked paprika
- ✓ 1 tsp cayenne pepper
- ✓ 1 pinch saffron thread
- ✓ 1/4 C. lemon juice
- ✓ 1 C. olive oil
- ✓ 1 tbsp kosher salt
- ✓ 6 boneless rib-eye steaks, excess fat trimmed, cubed
- ✓ 2 red onions, chopped
- ✓ 2 red bell peppers, chopped

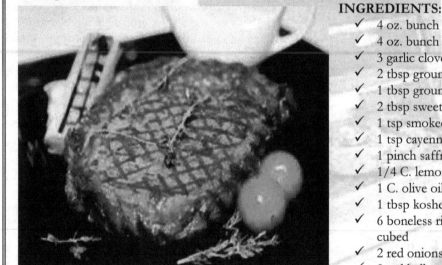

DIRECTIONS:

- ➤ Get a blender: Place in it the parsley with cilantro, garlic, cumin, coriander, paprika, cayenne, and saffron.
- ➤ Process them until them until they become smooth.
- ➤ Combine in the olive oil with lemon juice and salt. Blend them smooth to make the marinade.
- ➤ Get a mixing bowl: Stir in it the steak cubes with half of the marinade.
- ➤ Cover the bowl and let it sit in the fridge for 120 min.
- ➤ Before you do anything, preheat the grill and grease it.
- ➤ Thread the steak cubes with onion and peppers onto skewers while alternating between them.
- ➤ Grill them for 7 to 8 min on each side.
- ➤ Serve your steak skewers warm with the remaining marinade.
- ➤ Enjoy.

62 LAGUNA LUNCH WRAPS

Servings: 6　　　　　**Cook Time: 20 Min**　　　　　**Prep Time 15 Min**

INGREDIENTS:

- ✓ 2 tbsp olive oil
- ✓ 8 boneless skinless chicken thighs
- ✓ 1 sweet onion
- ✓ 1 cucumber
- ✓ 8 oz. Monterey jack and cheddar cheese blend
- ✓ 6 slices turkey bacon
- ✓ 16 oz. shredded lettuce ranch salad dressing
- ✓ 6 (10 inches) flour tortillas
- ✓ 1 lime

DIRECTIONS:

- ➢ Place a pan over medium heat. Heat in it the oil.
- ➢ Slice the chicken thighs into strips. Season them with a pinch of salt and pepper.
- ➢ Cook them in the hot oil for 8 to 10 min until they are done
- ➢ Drain them and place them aside.
- ➢ Place a small pan over medium heat. Cook in it the bacon until it becomes crisp.
- ➢ Drain it and place it aside.
- ➢ Heat the tortillas in a pan or microwave
- ➢ Lay them on a cutting board.
- ➢ Top them with ranch, lettuce, cucumbers, onion, bacon, cheese.
- ➢ Arrange the chicken strips on top followed by some lime juice.
- ➢ Wrap the tortillas and toast them on a grill or pan
- ➢ Grill for 2 to 3 min on each side. Serve them warm.
- ➢ Enjoy.

63 A WHOLE CHICKEN IN BELIZE

Servings: 3　　　　　**Cook Time: 30 Min**　　　　　**Prep Time 15 Min**

INGREDIENTS:

- ✓ 1/3 C. soy sauce
- ✓ 2 tbsp lime juice
- ✓ 5 garlic cloves
- ✓ 2 tsp ground cumin
- ✓ 1 tsp paprika
- ✓ 1/2 tsp dried oregano
- ✓ 1 tbsp vegetable oil
- ✓ 1 whole chicken, quartered

DIRECTIONS:

- ➢ Get a food processor: Combine in it the soy sauce, lime juice
- ➢ Add garlic, cumin, paprika, oregano, 1/2 tsp pepper, and oil.
- ➢ Get a large zip lock bag: place in it the chicken pieces. Pour over it the marinade.
- ➢ Seal the bag and let it sit in the fridge for 7 h to 26 h.
- ➢ Before you do anything, preheat the grill and grease it.
- ➢ Grill the chicken pieces for 15 to 18 min on each side. Serve them warm.
- ➢ Enjoy.

64 PERSIAN FRUIT BOWLS

Servings: 6   **Cook Time: 10 Min**   **Prep Time 13 Min**

INGREDIENTS:

- ✓ 1/3 C. honey
- ✓ 1 tbsp water
- ✓ 2 tsp orange blossom water

- ✓ 9 medium figs, stems trimmed and halved lengthwise
- ✓ 1-quart yogurt
- ✓ 1/3 C. pistachios, roasted, salted and chopped

DIRECTIONS:

- ➢ Before you do anything, preheat the grill and grease it.
- ➢ Get a mixing bowl: Whisk in it the honey, water, and orange blossom water.
- ➢ Before you do anything, preheat the grill and grease it.
- ➢ Place the figs on a baking tray. Coat them with the honey mixture.

- ➢ Lay them on the grill and put on the lid.
- ➢ Let them cook for 2 to 3 min while basting them with the leftover honey mixture.
- ➢ Turn over the figs and cook them for an extra 1 to 2 min.
- ➢ Garnish your grilled figs with pistachios. Serve them with some ice cream.
- ➢ Enjoy

65 TOPPED SEAFOOD TACOS

Servings: 2   **Cook Time: 3 Min**   **Prep Time 10 Min**

INGREDIENTS:

SAUCE

- ✓ 1 large avocado, chopped
- ✓ 1/2 C. water
- ✓ 1/4 C. loosely packed cilantro
- ✓ 1/2-1 large pickled jalapeno pepper, seeded
- ✓ 1 tbsp fresh limes
- ✓ 1 large garlic clove kosher salt

TACOS

- ✓ 4 -6 large sea scallops olive oil
- ✓ 1/2 C. green cabbage, sliced
- ✓ 1/4 C. red onion, sliced

- ✓ Black pepper Marinade
- ✓ 1 tbsp olive oil
- ✓ 1/2 limes, zest
- ✓ 1 tbsp limes
- ✓ 1 garlic clove, minced kosher salt
- ✓ Pepper

- ✓ 1 -1 1/2 tbsp cilantro, chopped
- ✓ 4 corn tortilla

DIRECTIONS:

- ➢ Get a food processor: Combine it all the sauce ingredients.
- ➢ Blend them smooth to make the sauce
- ➢ Get a mixing bowl: Whisk in it the marinade ingredients.
- ➢ Cut each scallop in half. Stir into it into the marinade
- ➢ Put on the lid and chill it in the fridge for 16 min.
- ➢ Get a mixing bowl: Combine in it the cabbage with onion and cilantro.
- ➢ Place a large pan over medium heat. Hat in it the olive oil.

- ➢ Drain the scallops from the marinade
- ➢ Cook them in the hot oil for 40 sec to 1 min on each side.
- ➢ Heat the tortillas in a pan or a microwave
- ➢ Place them on serving plates.
- ➢ Top each one of them with the cabbage salad, scallops, and avocado sauce.
- ➢ Wrap your tortillas then toast them in a grill pan or a grill.
- ➢ Serve them warm.
- ➢ Enjoy

67 EASY PORK CHUCK ROAST

Servings: 6   **Cook Time: 4 Min**   **Prep Time 15 Min**

INGREDIENTS:

- ✓ 1 whole 4-5 pounds chuck roast
- ✓ 1/4 cup olive oil
- ✓ 1/4 cup firm packed brown sugar
- ✓ 2 tablespoons Cajun seasoning
- ✓ 2 tablespoons paprika
- ✓ 2 tablespoons cayenne pepper

DIRECTIONS:

- ➢ Preheat smoker to 225 degrees Fahrenheit using oak wood
- ➢ Rub chuck roast all over with olive oil
- ➢ Take a small bowl and add brown sugar, paprika, Cajun seasoning, cayenne
- ➢ Coat the roast generously with the spice mix
- ➢ Transfer the chuck roast to smoker rack and smoke for 4-5 hours
- ➢ Once the internal temperature reaches 165°F, take the meat out and slice
- ➢ Enjoy!

68 PINEAPPLE PORK BBQ

Servings: 4   **Cook Time: 60 Min**   **Prep Time 10 Min**

INGREDIENTS:

- ✓ 1-Pound Pork Sirloin
- ✓ 4 Cups Pineapple Juice
- ✓ 3 Cloves Garlic, Minced
- ✓ 1 Cup Carne Aside Marinade
- ✓ 2 Tablespoons Salt
- ✓ 1 Teaspoon Ground Black pepper

DIRECTIONS:

- ➢ Place all ingredients in a bowl
- ➢ Massage the pork sirloin to coat with all elements
- ➢ Place inside the fridge to marinate for at least 2 hours.
- ➢ When ready to cook, fire the grill to 300F
- ➢ Use desired wood pellets when cooking the ribs
- ➢ Close the lid & preheat for 15 minutes.
- ➢ Place the pork sirloin on the grill grate and cook for 45 to 60 minutes
- ➢ Make sure to flip the pork halfway through the cooking time.
- ➢ At the same time, when you put the pork on the grill grate
- ➢ Place the marinade in a pan and place it inside the smoker
- ➢ Allow the marinade to cook and reduce.
- ➢ Baste the pork sirloin with the reduced marinade before the cooking time ends.
- ➢ Allow resting before slicing.

69 BBQ SPARERIBS WITH MANDARIN GLAZE

Servings: 6   **Cook Time: 1 H**   **Prep Time 10 Min**

INGREDIENTS:
- ✓ 3 large spareribs, membrane removed
- ✓ 3 tablespoons yellow mustard
- ✓ 1 tablespoon Worcestershire sauce
- ✓ 1 cup honey
- ✓ 1 1/2 cup brown sugar
- ✓ 13 ounces Trailer Mandarin Glaze
- ✓ 1 teaspoon sesame oil
- ✓ 1 teaspoon soy sauce
- ✓ 1 teaspoon garlic powder

DIRECTIONS:
- ➤ Place the spareribs on a working surface and carefully
- ➤ Remove the connective tissue membrane that covers the ribs.
- ➤ Set the rest of the ingredients until well combined in a bowl.
- ➤ Massage the spice mixture onto the spareribs
- ➤ Allow resting in the fridge for at least 3 hours.
- ➤ When ready to cook, fire the grill to 300F.
- ➤ Close the lid & preheat for 15 minutes.
- ➤ Place the seasoned ribs on the grill grate and cover the lid.
- ➤ Cook for 60 minutes.
- ➤ Once cooked, allow resting before slicing.

70 SMOKED PORK SAUSAGES

Servings: 6   **Cook Time: 1 H**   **Prep Time 10 Min**

INGREDIENTS:
- ✓ 3 pounds ground pork
- ✓ 1/2 tablespoon ground mustard
- ✓ 1 tablespoon onion powder
- ✓ 1 tablespoon garlic powder
- ✓ 1 teaspoon pink curing salt
- ✓ 1 teaspoon salt
- ✓ 1 teaspoon black pepper
- ✓ 1/4 cup of ice water
- ✓ Hog casings, soaked & rinsed in cold water

DIRECTIONS:
- ➤ Mix all ingredients except for the hog casings in a bowl
- ➤ Use your hands, mix until all ingredients are well-combined.
- ➤ Apply a sausage stuffer, stuff the hog casings with the pork mixture.
- ➤ Measure 4 inches of the stuffed hog casing and twist to form into a sausage
- ➤ Repeat the process until you create sausage links.
- ➤ When ready to cook, fire the grill to 225F
- ➤ Make use of apple wood pellets when cooking the ribs
- ➤ Close the lid & preheat for 15 minutes.
- ➤ Place the sausage links on the grill grate
- ➤ Cook for 1 hour or until the sausage's internal temperature reads at 155F.
- ➤ Allow resting before slicing.

71 BRAISED PORK CHILE VERDE

Servings: 6 **Cook Time: 40 Min** **Prep Time 10 Min**

INGREDIENTS:

- ✓ 3 pounds pork shoulder, bone removed and cut into 1/2 inch cubes
- ✓ 1 tablespoon all-purpose flour
- ✓ Salt and pepper to taste
- ✓ 1-pound tomatillos, husked and washed
- ✓ 2 jalapenos, chopped
- ✓ 1 medium yellow onion and peeled then cut into chunks

- ✓ 4 cloves of garlic
- ✓ 4 tablespoons extra virgin olive oil
- ✓ 2 cup chicken stock
- ✓ 2 cans green chilies 1 tablespoon cumin
- ✓ 1 tablespoon oregano 1/2 lime, juiced
- ✓ 1/4 cup cilantro

DIRECTIONS:

- ➢ Place the pork shoulder chunks in a bowl and toss with flour
- ➢ Season with salt and pepper to taste.
- ➢ Use desired wood pellets when cooking
- ➢ Place a large cast-iron skillet on the bottom rack of the grill
- ➢ Close the lid & preheat for 15 minutes.
- ➢ Put the tomatillos, jalapeno, onion, and garlic on a sheet tray
- ➢ lined with foil and drizzle with 2 tablespoon olive oil
- ➢ Season with salt and pepper to taste.
- ➢ Place the remaining olive oil in the heated cast iron
- ➢ skillet and cook the pork shoulder

- ➢ Spread the meat evenly, then close.
- ➢ Before closing the lid, place the vegetables in the tray on the grill rack
- ➢ Close the lid of the grill.
- ➢ Cook for 20 minutes w/o opening the lid or stirring the pork
- ➢ Pulse until smooth and pour into the pan with the pork
- ➢ Stir in the chicken stock, green chilies, cumin, oregano, and lime juice
- ➢ Season with salt and pepper to taste
- ➢ Close the grill lid & cook for another 20 minutes
- ➢ Once cooked, stir in the cilantro.

72 FULLY GRILLED STEAK

Servings: 2 **Cook Time: 15 Min** **Prep Time 60 Min**

INGREDIENTS:

- ✓ 2 USDA Choice or Prime 11/4-11/2 Inch New York Strip Steak (Approx. 12-14 ounces each)

- ✓ Extra Virgin Olive Oil
- ✓ 4 teaspoons of Western Love or Salt and Pepper

DIRECTIONS:

- ➢ Remove the steak from the refrigerator
- ➢ Loosely cover with wrap about 45 minutes before returning to room temperature.
- ➢ When the steak reaches room temperature, polish both sides with olive oil.
- ➢ Season from each side of the steak with a teaspoon of rub or salt and pepper
- ➢ Absorb at room temperature for at least 5 minutes before grilling.
- ➢ Configure a wood pellet smoker and grill for direct cooking using a baking grate
- ➢ Set the temperature high, and preheat to at least 450° F using the pellets.
- ➢ Place steak on grill & cook for 2-3 minutes until browned on one side.

- ➢ On the same side, rotate the steak 90 degrees to mark the cross grill and cook for another 2-3 minutes
- ➢ Turn the steak over and bake until the desired finish is achieved.
- ➢ 3-5 minutes for medium-rare (135 ° F internal temperature)
- ➢ 6-7 minutes for medium (140 ° F internal temperature)
- ➢ 8-10 minutes for medium wells (internal temperature 150 ° F)
- ➢ Transfer the steak to a platter, loosen the tent with foil and leave for 5 minutes before serving.

74 SMOKED ROAST BEEF

Servings: 8   **Cook Time: 14 H**   **Prep Time 10 Min**

INGREDIENTS:
- ✓ 1 (4-pound) top round roast
- ✓ 1 batch Espresso Brisket Rub
- ✓ 1 tablespoon butter

DIRECTIONS:
- ➤ Supply your smoker w/ wood pellets and follow the manufacturer's specific start-up procedure
- ➤ Allow your griller to preheat with the lid closed, to 180°F.
- ➤ Season the top round roast with the rub
- ➤ Use your two hands, work the rub into the meat.
- ➤ Place the meat to roast directly on the grill grate
- ➤ Smoke until its internal temperature reaches 140°F
- ➤ Remove the roast from the grill.
- ➤ Place a cast-iron skillet on the grill grate and increase the grill's temperature to 450°F
- ➤ Put the roast in the skillet, add the butter, and cook until its internal temperature reaches 145°F, flipping once after about 3 minutes
- ➤ (It is recommended to sear the meat over an open flame rather than in the cast iron skillet if your grill has this option)
- ➤ Remove the food you roast from the grill
- ➤ Let it rest for 10 to 15 minutes before slicing and serving.

75 PULLED BEEF

Servings: 5   **Cook Time: 14 H**   **Prep Time 25 Min**

INGREDIENTS:
- ✓ 1 (4-pound) top round roast
- ✓ 2 tablespoons yellow mustard
- ✓ 1 batch Espresso Brisket Rub
- ✓ 1/2 cup beef broth

DIRECTIONS:
- ➤ Supply your smoker w/ wood pellets and follow the manufacturer's specific start-up procedure
- ➤ Allow your griller to preheat with the lid closed to have quality food to 225°F.
- ➤ Coat the top round roast all over with mustard
- ➤ Season it with the rub. Using your two hands, work the rub into the meat.
- ➤ Place the meat to roast directly on the grill grate and smoke until its internal temperature reaches 160°F and a dark bark has formed.
- ➤ Pull the roast from the grill and place it on enough aluminum foil to wrap it completely.
- ➤ Increase the grill's temperature to 350°F.
- ➤ Fold in three sides of the foil around the roast and add the beef broth
- ➤ Pleat in the last side, completely enclosing the roast and liquid
- ➤ Return the wrapped roast to the grill
- ➤ Cook until its internal temperature reaches 195°F.
- ➤ Pull the roast from the grill and place it in a cooler
- ➤ Cover the cooler and let the roast rest for 1 or 2 hours.
- ➤ Remove your roast from the cooler and unwrap it
- ➤ Extract apart the beef using just your fingers. Serve immediately.

76 ALMOND CRUSTED BEEF FILLET

Servings: 4　　　　　**Cook Time: 55 Min**　　　　　**Prep Time 15 Min**

INGREDIENTS:

- ✓ 1/4 cup chopped almonds
- ✓ 1 tablespoon Dijon mustard
- ✓ 1 cup chicken broth
- ✓ Salt
- ✓ 1/3 cup chopped onion
- ✓ 1/4 cup olive oil Pepper
- ✓ 2 tablespoons curry powder
- ✓ 3 Pounds beef fillet tenderloin

DIRECTIONS:

- ➢ Rub the pepper and salt into the tenderloin.
- ➢ Place the almonds, mustard, chicken broth, curry, onion, and olive oil into a bowl
- ➢ Stir well to combine.
- ➢ Take this mixture and rub the tenderloin generously with it.
- ➢ Add wood pellets to your smoker and follow your cooker's startup procedure
- ➢ Preheat your smoker, with your lid closed, until it reaches 450.
- ➢ Lie on the grill, cover, and smoke for ten minutes on both sides.
- ➢ Continue to cook until it reaches your desired doneness.
- ➢ Take the entire grill and let it rest for at least ten minutes.

77 BALSAMIC VINEGAR MOLASSES STEAK

Servings: 4　　　　　**Cook Time: 20 Min**　　　　　**Prep Time 15 Min**

INGREDIENTS:

- ✓ Pepper Salt
- ✓ 1 tablespoon balsamic vinegar
- ✓ 2 tablespoons molasses

- ✓ 1 tablespoon red wine vinegar
- ✓ 1 cup beef broth
- ✓ 1/2 pounds steak of choice

DIRECTIONS:

- ➢ Lay the steaks in a zip-top bag.
- ➢ Add the balsamic vinegar, red wine vinegar, molasses, and beef broth to a bowl. Combine thoroughly by stirring.
- ➢ On the top of the steaks, drizzle this mixture.
- ➢ Place into the refrigerator for eight hours.
- ➢ Add wood pellets to your smoker and follow your cooker's startup procedure

- ➢ Preheat your smoker, with your lid closed, until it reaches 350.
- ➢ Take the flounced steaks out of the refrigerator 30 minutes before you are ready to grill.
- ➢ Put on the grill, cover, and smoke for ten minutes per side, or until meat is tender.
- ➢ Place onto plates and let them rest for ten minutes.

78 HERBED STEAKS

Servings: 4   **Cook Time: 30 Min**   **Prep Time 10 Min**

INGREDIENTS:
- ✓ Pinch red pepper flakes
- ✓ 1/2 teaspoon coriander seeds
- ✓ 2 teaspoons green peppercorns
- ✓ 2 teaspoons black peppercorns
- ✓ 2 tablespoons chopped mint leaves
- ✓ 1/4 cup olive oil
- ✓ 2 tablespoons peanut oil
- ✓ 3 pounds flank steak

DIRECTIONS:
- ➢ Sprinkle the flank steak with salt and rub generously
- ➢ Lay the meat in a large zip-top bag.
- ➢ Mix together the red pepper flakes, coriander, peppercorns, mint leaves, olive oil, and peanut oil.
- ➢ Pour this mixture over the flank steak.
- ➢ Place into the refrigerator for four hours.
- ➢ Add wood pellets to your smoker and follow your cooker's startup procedure
- ➢ Preheat your smoker, with your lid closed, until it reaches 450.

- ➢ Take the flank steak out of the refrigerator 30 minutes before you are ready to grill it.
- ➢ Put the flank steak onto the grill and grill ten minutes on each
- ➢ (You can grill longer if you want the steak more well done)
- ➢ After removing from the grill and set for about ten minutes
- ➢ Slice before serving.

79 BEER HONEY STEAKS

Servings: 4   **Cook Time: 30 Min**   **Prep Time 10 Min**

INGREDIENTS:
- ✓ Pepper
- ✓ Juice of one lemon
- ✓ 1 cup beer of choice
- ✓ 1 tablespoon honey
- ✓ Salt
- ✓ 2 tablespoons olive oil
- ✓ 1 teaspoon thyme
- ✓ 4 steaks of choice

DIRECTIONS:
- ➢ Season the steaks with pepper and salt.
- ➢ Combine together the olive oil, lemon juice, honey, thyme, and beer.
- ➢ Rub the steaks with this mixture generously.
- ➢ Add wood pellets to your smoker and follow your cooker's startup procedure

- ➢ Preheat your smoker, with your lid closed, until it reaches 450.
- ➢ Place the steaks onto the grill, cover, and smoke for ten minutes per side.
- ➢ For about 10 minutes, let it cool after removing it from the grill.

80 LA ROCHELLE STEAK

Servings: 4   **Cook Time: 20 Min**   **Prep Time 10 Min**

INGREDIENTS:

- ✓ 1 tablespoon red currant jelly
- ✓ 1/2 teaspoon salt
- ✓ 3 teaspoon curry powder
- ✓ 8 ounces pineapple chunks in juice
- ✓ 1 1/2 pounds flank steak
- ✓ 1/4 cup olive oil

DIRECTIONS:

- ➤ Put the flank steak into a large bag.
- ➤ Mix the pepper, salt, red currant jelly, curry powder, pineapple chunks with juice and olive oil.
- ➤ Pour this mixture over the flank steak.
- ➤ Place into the refrigerator for four hours.
- ➤ Add wood pellets to your smoker and follow your cooker's startup procedure
- ➤ Preheat your smoker, with your lid closed, until it reaches 350.

- ➤ Then you are ready to cook the steak
- ➤ Remove the steak from the refrigerator 30 minutes before ready to cook.
- ➤ Lay the steaks on the grill, cover, and smoke for ten minutes on both sides, or done to your liking.
- ➤ Remove your roasted food from the grill and allow cooling for about ten minutes.

81 SPICED BRISKET

Servings: 8   **Cook Time: 9 H**   **Prep Time 10 Min**

INGREDIENTS:

- ✓ 2 tablespoons onion powder
- ✓ 2 tablespoons garlic powder
- ✓ 2 teaspoons chili powder
- ✓ 2 tablespoons paprika
- ✓ 1/3 cup coarse ground black pepper
- ✓ 1/3 cup Jacobsen salt
- ✓ Brisket:
- ✓ 1 (12 to 14 pounds / 5.4 to 6.4 kg) whole packer brisket, trimmed
- ✓ 11/2 cup beef broth

DIRECTIONS:

- ➤ Thoroughly put all the rub ingredients. Season the brisket with the rub on all sides.
- ➤ When ready to cook, set grill temperature to 225°F (107°C)
- ➤ Preheat, lid closed for 15 minutes. For optimal flavor, use Super Smoke if available.
- ➤ Place the brisket, fat-side down, on the grill and cook for about 5 to 6 hours.

- ➤ Take out the brisket and wrap in a double layer of foil, then add the beef broth to the foil packet.
- ➤ Return the foiled brisket to the grill and cook for about another 3 hours.
- ➤ Take out the brisket and unwrap from foil. Allow resting for 15 minutes

82 LEMON CHICKEN IN FOIL PACKET

Servings: 4   **Cook Time: 25 Min**   **Prep Time 5 Min**

INGREDIENTS:
- ✓ Four chicken fillets
- ✓ Three tablespoons melted butter
- ✓ One garlic, minced
- ✓ 1-1/2 teaspoon dried Italian seasoning
- ✓ Salt and pepper to taste
- ✓ One lemon, sliced

DIRECTIONS:
- ➤ Turn on your wood pellet grill.
- ➤ Keep the lid open while burning for 5 minutes.
- ➤ Preheat it to 450 degrees F.
- ➤ Add the chicken fillet on top of foil sheets.
- ➤ In a bowl, mix the butter, garlic, seasoning, salt, and pepper.
- ➤ Brush the chicken with this mixture.
- ➤ Put the lemon slices on top.
- ➤ Wrap the chicken with the foil.
- ➤ Grill each side for 7 to 10 minutes per side.

83 SWEET AND SPICY CHICKEN

Servings: 4   **Cook Time: 40 Min**   **Prep Time 30 Min**

INGREDIENTS:
- ✓ 16 chicken wings
- ✓ Three tablespoons lime juice
- ✓ A sweet, spicy rub

DIRECTIONS:
- ➤ Arrange chicken wings in a baking pan.
- ➤ Pour the lime juice over the wings.
- ➤ Sprinkle the wings with the seasoning.
- ➤ Set your wood pellet grill to 350 degrees F.
- ➤ Add the chicken wings to the grill.
- ➤ Grill for 20 minutes per side.

84 GRILLED CHICKEN

Servings: 6   **Cook Time: 1 H 10 Min**   **Prep Time 30 Min**

INGREDIENTS:
- ✓ 5 lb. whole chicken
- ✓ 1/2 cup oil
- ✓ Trigger chicken rub

DIRECTIONS:
- ➤ Preheat the grill with the lid open for 5 minutes
- ➤ Close the lid, and let it warm for 15 minutes or until it reaches 450.
- ➤ Use bakers' twine to tie the chicken legs together
- ➤ Then rub it with oil. Coat the chicken with the rub and place it on the grill.
- ➤ Grill for 70 minutes with the lid closed
- ➤ (Or until it reaches an internal temperature of 1650F)
- ➤ Remove the chicken from the grill and let rest for 15 minutes
- ➤ Cut and serve.

85 SPECIAL OCCASION'S DINNER CORNISH HEN

Servings: 4 **Cook Time: 1 H** **Prep Time 15 Min**

INGREDIENTS:
- ✓ 4 Cornish game hens
- ✓ Four fresh rosemary sprigs
- ✓ 4 Tbsp. butter, melted
- ✓ 4 Tsp. chicken rub

DIRECTIONS:
- ➤ Set the grill temperature to 375 degrees F and preheat with a closed lid for 15 minutes.
- ➤ With paper towels, pat dries the hens.
- ➤ Tuck the wings behind the backs, and with kitchen strings, tie the legs together.
- ➤ Coat the outside of each hen with melted butter and sprinkle with rub evenly.
- ➤ Set each hen with a rosemary sprig.
- ➤ Place the hens onto the grill and cook for about 50-60 minutes.
- ➤ Remove the hens from your grill and put onto a platter for about 10 minutes.
- ➤ Cut each hen into desired-sized pieces and serve.

86 CRISPY AND JUICY CHICKEN

Servings: 6 **Cook Time: 5 H** **Prep Time 15 Min**

INGREDIENTS:
- ✓ 3/4 C. dark brown sugar
- ✓ 1/2 C. ground espresso beans
- ✓ 1 Tbsp. ground cumin
- ✓ 1 Tbsp. ground cinnamon
- ✓ 1 Tbsp. garlic powder
- ✓ 1 Tbsp. cayenne pepper
- ✓ Salt and freshly ground black pepper
- ✓ (4-lb.) whole chicken, neck and giblets removed

DIRECTIONS:
- ➤ Set the grill temperature to 200-225 degrees F and preheat with a closed lid for 15 minutes.
- ➤ In a bowl, mix brown sugar, ground espresso, spices, salt, and black pepper.
- ➤ Rub the chicken with spice mixture generously.
- ➤ Put the chicken onto the grill and cook for about 3-5 hours.
- ➤ Remove chicken from grill and place onto a cutting board for about 10 minutes before carving.
- ➤ W/ a sharp knife cut the chicken into desired sized pieces and serve.

87 DRUMSTICKS

Servings: 6 **Cook Time: 3 H**

Prep Time 15 Min

INGREDIENTS:
- ✓ 1 C. fresh orange juice
- ✓ 1/4 C. honey
- ✓ 2 Tbsp. sweet chili sauce
- ✓ 2 Tbsp. hoisin sauce
- ✓ 2 Tbsp. fresh ginger, grated finely
- ✓ 2 Tbsp. garlic, minced
- ✓ 1 Tsp. Sriracha
- ✓ 1/2 Tsp. sesame oil
- ✓ Six chicken drumsticks

DIRECTIONS:
- ➤ Set the condition of the grill to 225 degrees F.
- ➤ Preheat with a closed lid for 15 minutes.
- ➤ In a bowl, place all fixings except for chicken drumsticks and mix until well combined.
- ➤ Reserve half of the honey mixture in a small bowl.
- ➤ In the bowl of the remaining sauce, add drumsticks and mix well.
- ➤ Arrange the chicken drumsticks onto the grill
- ➤ Cook for about 3 hours, basting with remaining sauce occasionally.
- ➤ Serve hot.

88 CAJUN PATCH COCK CHICKEN

Servings: 4 **Cook Time: 2 H 30 Min** **Prep Time 3H 30 Min**

INGREDIENTS:

- ✓ 4-5 pounds of fresh or thawed flounced chicken
- ✓ 4-6 glasses of extra virgin olive oil
- ✓ Cajun Spice Lab 4 tablespoons or Lucile Bloody Mary Mix Cajun Hot Dry Herb Mix Seasoning

DIRECTIONS:

- ➢ Take the chicken on a cutting board with the chest down.
- ➢ Use kitchen or poultry scissors, cut along the side of the spine and remove.
- ➢ Turn the chicken over & press down firmly on the chest to flatten it. Carefully loosen
- ➢ Remove the skin on the chest, thighs and drumsticks.
- ➢ Smoke chicken for 1.5 hours.
- ➢ After one and a half hours at 225 ° F, raise the pit temperature to 375 ° F
- ➢ Place the chicken under a loose foil tent for 15 minutes before carving.

89 MONTEREY CHICKEN

Servings: 8 **Cook Time: 20 Min** **Prep Time 5 Min**

INGREDIENTS:

- ✓ 4 Chicken Breast (boneless/skinless)
- ✓ 2ounce Grande Gringo Mexican Seasoning
- ✓ 12ounce Bacon (crumbled)
- ✓ 4ounce Monterey Jack Cheese
- ✓ 4ounce Sharp Cheddar Cheese
- ✓ 1 cup Killer Hogs BBQ Sauce
- ✓ 2 to 3 Green Onions (chopped)

DIRECTIONS:

- ➢ Get ready pellet flame broil for cooking at 325.
- ➢ Season the chicken bosom with the Grande Gringo Mexican flavoring on all sides.
- ➢ Spot the bosoms on the pellet flame broil embed a test thermometer to screen inner temperature.
- ➢ When the inside temp arrives at 155, exchange the chicken bosoms to a level iron skillet
- ➢ Coat with Killer Hogs BBQ Sauce. Keep on cooking the bosoms until the inner arrives at 165.
- ➢ Top each bosom with disintegrated bacon, cheddar, and jack cheddar. Return the skillet to the barbecue
- ➢ Cook for 3 to 5minutes or until the cheddar liquefies over the top.
- ➢ Enhance the Monterey Chicken with green onions and serve.

90 EASY RAPID-FIRE ROAST CHICKEN

Servings: 4 **Cook Time: 1 H 30 Min** **Prep Time 10 Min**

INGREDIENTS:

- ✓ 1 (4-pound) whole chicken, giblets removed
- ✓ Extra-virgin olive oil, for rubbing
- ✓ 3 tablespoons Greek seasoning
- ✓ Juice of 1 lemon
- ✓ Butcher's string

DIRECTIONS:

- ➢ Supply your smoker w/ wood pellets and follow the manufacturer's specific start-up procedure
- ➢ Preheat, with the lid, closed, to 450°F.
- ➢ Rub the bird generously all over with oil, including inside the cavity.
- ➢ Put the chicken directly on the grill, breast-side up, close the lid, and roast.
- ➢ Let the meat rest for 10 minutes before carving.

91 CINCH DE MAYO CHICKEN ENCHILADAS

Servings: 6 **Cook Time: 45 Min** **Prep Time 15 Min**

INGREDIENTS:

- ✓ 6 cups diced cooked chicken
- ✓ 3 cups grated Monterey Jack cheese, divided
- ✓ 1 cup sour cream
- ✓ 1 (4-ounce) can be chopped green chills
- ✓ 2 (10-ounce) cans red, divided
- ✓ 12 (8-inch) flour tortillas
- ✓ 1/2 cup chopped scallions
- ✓ 1/4 cup chopped fresh cilantro

DIRECTIONS:

- ➤ Supply your smoker w/ wood pellets and follow the manufacturer's specific start-up procedure
- ➤ Preheat, with the lid, closed, to 350°F.
- ➤ In a large bowl, combine the cooked chicken, 2 cups of cheese, the sour cream, and green chills to fill.
- ➤ Bake on the grill, w/ the lid closed, for 30 minutes, and then remove the foil.
- ➤ Continue baking with the lid closed for 15 minutes, or until bubbly.
- ➤ Garnish the enchiladas with the chopped scallions and cilantro and serve immediately.

92 MINI TURDUCKEN ROULADE

Servings: 6 **Cook Time: 2 H**

Prep Time 20 Min

INGREDIENTS:

- ✓ 1 (16-ounce) boneless turkey breast
- ✓ 1 (8-to 10-ounce) boneless duck breast
- ✓ 1 (8-ounce) boneless, skinless chicken breast
- ✓ Salt
- ✓ Freshly ground black pepper
- ✓ 2 cups Italian dressing
- ✓ 2 tablespoons Cajun seasoning
- ✓ 1 cup prepared seasoned stuffing mix
- ✓ 8 slices bacon
- ✓ Butcher's string
- ✓ Butterfly the turkey, duck, and chicken breasts cover plastic wrap and, using a mallet, flatten each 1/2 inch thick

DIRECTIONS:

- ➤ Season all the meat on both sides with a little salt and pepper.
- ➤ In a medium bowl, combine the Italian dressing and Cajun seasoning
- ➤ Spread one-fourth of the mixture on top of the flattened turkey breast.
- ➤ Place the turducken roulade in a roasting pan
- ➤ Take to the grill and roast for 2 hours
- ➤ (Or until a meat thermometer inserted in the turducken reads 165°F)
- ➤ Tent with aluminum foil in the last 30 minutes, if necessary, to keep from over-browning.
- ➤ Let the turducken rest for 15 to 20 minutes before carving. Serve warm.

93 TURKEY LEGS

Servings: 5   **Cook Time: 5 H**   **Prep Time 10 Min**

INGREDIENTS:

✓ 4 turkey legs

FOR THE BRINE:

✓ 1/2 cup curing salt
✓ 1 tablespoon whole black peppercorns
✓ 1 cup BBQ rub
✓ 1/2 cup brown sugar
✓ 2 bay leaves

✓ 2 teaspoons liquid smoke
✓ 16 cups of warm water
✓ 4 cups ice
✓ 8 cups of cold water

DIRECTIONS:

➤ Prepare the brine and for this, take a large stockpot
➤ Place it over high heat, pour warm water in it, add peppercorn, bay leaves, and liquid smoke
➤ Stir in salt, sugar, and BBQ rub and bring it to a boil
➤ Remove pot from heat, bring it to room temperature
➤ Then pour in cold water, add ice cubes and let the brine chill in the refrigerator.
➤ At this point add turkey legs in it, submerge them completely
➤ Let soak for 24 hours in the refrigerator.
➤ After 24 hours, remove turkey legs from the brine

➤ Rinse well and pat dry with paper towels.
➤ When ready to cook, switch on the grill, fill the grill hopper with hickory flavored wood pellets
➤ Power the grill on by using the control panel
➤ Select 'smoke' on the temperature dial, or set the temperature to 250 degrees F
➤ Let it preheat for a minimum of 15 minutes.
➤ When the grill has preheated, open the lid
➤ Put turkey legs on the grill grate, shut the grill, and smoke for 5 hours
➤ (Until nicely browned and the internal temperature reaches 165 degrees F)
➤ Serve immediately.

94 SPATCHCOCK TURKEY

Servings: 12   **Cook Time: 1 H 20 Min**   **Prep Time 20 Min**

INGREDIENTS:

FOR TURKEY

✓ 1 whole turkey (roughly 15 pounds), thawed
✓ Salt to taste

FOR TURKEY STOCK INGREDIENTS 4 CARROTS, SLICED

✓ 4 carrots, sliced
✓ 1 onion, chopped
✓ 5 spring's fresh thyme
✓ 1-quart unsalted chicken stock
✓ 5 spring's fresh sage
✓ 1-quart water
✓ 4 stalks of celery, chopped

DIRECTIONS:

➤ Cut out the backbone using kitchen shears or a sharp knife & set aside.
➤ Lay the turkey flat on a metallic rack & generously practice the dry brine on both sides (salt)
➤ Place in a refrigerator for a single day to air dry.
➤ Next, put the whole elements for turkey inventory in a large-sized roasting pan

➤ Place the roasting pan over the pellet grill & placed the top shelf in its place
➤ (Putting the turkey over the top shelf).
➤ Grill the turkey until the inner temperature displays 160 F, at 350 F.
➤ Strain the turkey stock & sense free to apply it in gravy. Serve warm and enjoy.

CPSIA information can be obtained
at www.ICGtesting.com
Printed in the USA
BVHW050041270421
605863BV00011B/1736